Leadership Pearls in Healthcare

Ralph Junckerstorff · Sara Baqar
Editors

Leadership Pearls in Healthcare

 Springer

Editors
Ralph Junckerstorff
General (Internal Medicine)
and Infectious Diseases
Monash Health
Melbourne, VIC, Australia

Sara Baqar
Department of Endocrinology
Austin Health
Melbourne, VIC, Australia

ISBN 978-981-96-4232-8   ISBN 978-981-96-4233-5   (eBook)
https://doi.org/10.1007/978-981-96-4233-5

This Springer imprint is published by the registered company Springer Nature Singapore Pte Ltd.
The registered company address is: 152 Beach Road, #21-01/04 Gateway East, Singapore 189721,
Singapore

If disposing of this product, please recycle the paper.

Contents

Editors and Contributors

About the Editors

Ralph Junckerstorff is a General (Internal) Medicine and Infectious Diseases physician at Monash Health in Melbourne, Victoria. He graduated from undergraduate medicine from the University of Western Australia in 2000 and became a fellow of the Royal Australasian College of Physicians in 2010. He also holds a Diploma of Tropical Medicine from the University of Liverpool (UK). He is a co-editor of the book *Beyond Evidence-Based Medicine: Clinical Pearls from Experienced Physicians*.

Dr Junckerstorff has worked in a public teaching hospital his entire career. He has shared an office with former and current Directors of General Medicine and is married to a healthcare leader. He fully appreciates how difficult, time-consuming and, at times, thankless a task being a leader is. He understands the complexities and challenges of the hospital environment and the significant impact effective leadership in healthcare can have.

Sara Baqar is an Endocrinologist and the first female Director of Endocrinology at Austin Health, Melbourne, Australia. She previously served as the Director of General Medicine at Monash Health and Northeast Health, Wangaratta.

Graduating from Monash University in 2003, her specialisation in endocrinology was complemented by receiving the National Heart Foundation Health Professional Scholarship and the University of Melbourne Faculty Research Scholarship, supporting her impactful PhD on salt's effects on diabetes and cardiovascular health.

Associate Professor Baqar is recognised for her international presentations, numerous publications and active involvement as the principal investigator in ongoing studies. Her varied contributions underscore a dedication to advancing medical knowledge, improving patient care and fostering the growth of future healthcare professionals.

Contributors

Sara Barnes is a Physician who has a passion for innovation and change. Sara is dedicated to examining hospital workflows to enhance patient care and workplace satisfaction in a cost-effective manner. Since her arrival at Monash Health, she has developed the Allergy service and is currently the Medical Lead of the Allergy/Immunology service, transforming it into the state centre for Venom Immunotherapy and a key referral centre for Vaccine Allergy. In collaboration with the quaternary maternity services at Monash Health, she leads the Allergy/Immunology service in providing expert advice for patients with adverse reactions to insulin and penicillins where treatment is required.

Sara completed her MBA at Deakin University in 2017, which has enabled her to design financially sustainable models of care. The Monash Health Allergy/Immunology unit places a strong emphasis on collaboration with other hospitals to explore innovative care models and research initiatives. Although Sara has participated in several multi-centre international studies, she is particularly passionate about analysing local workflow practices to align them with the best evidence to achieve optimal outcomes. The Monash Health unit has successfully published numerous findings related to these improvements in recent years.

Utilising her distinctive blend of business and medical expertise, Sara has served on the National Asthma Council Board of Directors and has actively participated in various committees and working groups at both local and national levels.

Describe the circumstances surrounding your first leadership position

About 10 years ago, someone suggested that I apply for a leadership programme that only accepts 30 people each year. I was surprised by this, as at that point, I didn't see myself as a leader. I am still figuring out what my own style of leadership is, but I have learned that there are many different ways to be a leader. I don't think I'll ever fully feel comfortable with the idea of being called a leader.

Don Campbell is the Medical Director, Design and Discovery Division, Northern Health in Melbourne, Australia. He is recognised internationally for contributions to healthcare reform and innovation using Systemic Design. He has a background in Respiratory and General Medicine and is a Past President of the Adult Medicine Division of the Royal Australasian College of Physicians and the Internal Medicine Society of Australia and New Zealand. He is currently implementing a novel programme for high-needs complex patients at Northern Health (Patient Watch).

He holds adjunct professorial appointments in both the Faculty of Medicine, Nursing, Health Sciences and Faculty of Art, Design and Architecture at Monash University. He has contributed over 100 peer-reviewed publications, with over 3000 citations, including 7 book chapters, 6 editorials, as well as invited contributions and internet publications and guidelines. He has been an invited Faculty member teaching Design Thinking on the Innovation in Healthcare and Education course with the Monash Institute of Health and Education (MIHCE) and Harvard Macy Institute (2016–2018). His current research grant support includes a randomised, placebo-controlled trial to investigate the efficacy of intranasal heparin treatment to reduce transmission of SARS-CoV-2 infection and COVID disease among household contacts of SARS-CoV-2+ adults and children (Victorian Government, $4.2M), and Emerging from the long shadow: Optimising supportive consumer and provider journeys through the post-acute sequelae of COVID-19 (Australian Government MRFF, $5 million).

Describe the circumstances surrounding your first leadership position

I was asked to come to the headmaster's office at the end of year 11 in secondary school. I was offered a cup of tea, then told/asked if I wanted to be School Captain and President of Student Representative Council the following year. I said yes, realising instantly that this meant a lot of work that I hadn't counted on. The role was not one that I desired or actively sought.

The offer was unexpected, and I did no preparation for the role. Expectations were laid down at the first meeting. I sought to involve others around me in the process and shared responsibilities for decisions and actions.

Allen Cheng is an infectious diseases physician, epidemiologist, and biostatistician. He is Professor/Director of Infectious Diseases at Monash Health and the School of Clinical Sciences at Monash University in Melbourne, Australia. He has interests in influenza and respiratory infections, infection control and antimicrobial resistance, and public health.

Describe the circumstances surrounding your first leadership position

My first leadership position as Director of Infection Prevention was a natural career progression from my previous work as a clinician and researcher. I had also over time, progressed from sitting on government committees to chairing them. But like many other infectious diseases physicians during the COVID-19 pandemic, I unexpectedly found myself in new and strange roles, including Acting Victorian Chief Health Officer and chairing and sitting on various government advisory committees.

Nick Coatsworth is one of Australia's foremost and widely recognised medical authority and public health communicators. His unique breadth of experience in the delivery of healthcare extends from frontline roles across four States and Territories to international humanitarian disasters. As a Deputy Chief Medical Officer of Australia during the COVID-19 pandemic, Nick's calm, clear communication supported the nation through one of its greatest health challenges. Nick's leadership in medicine has included senior roles in federal and state health departments and public hospitals. He has extensive experience in clinical governance and risk management at all levels of healthcare, implementing a range of quality and safety initiatives during his time at Canberra Health Services.

Dr Coatsworth became a leader in Australian humanitarian medicine through his early career work with Médecins Sans Frontières and Australian Medical Assistance Teams. He regularly lectures on health security at the National Security College and is conducting doctoral research exploring the crisis decision-making in the first 70 days of the pandemic at the Australian National University. Nick is a Fellow of the Royal Australian College of Physicians and is trained in both respiratory and infectious disease medicine. In 2022, the University of Western Australia, his alma mater, awarded him an Honorary Doctorate for his exceptional service to medicine. While maintaining a frontline presence as a clinician and educator at Canberra Hospital, Nick takes pride in being both a dedicated father and a keen hobby farmer.

Describe the circumstances surrounding your first leadership position

I brought together a young team of like-minded medical students and put in a bid for Executive of the Australian Medical Students Association in 1999. It was successful (because we were unopposed!) and I became President of the Association for a year. For me this symbolised the importance of saying 'yes' to, and seeking out leadership opportunities in healthcare, and taking on these roles as early as possible in one's career.

Barbora de Courten OAM is a Distinguished Professor at RMIT University, where she leads healthcare innovation as the Founding Director of the RMIT Centre for Health by Design. She also holds adjunct professorial appointments at Monash University and the University of Queensland and continues her clinical work as a Specialist Physician at Monash Health.

Barbora's academic journey spans epidemiology, clinical trials, and public health, with a PhD in epidemiology, a Master of Public Health, and advanced training in clinical trials from the National Institutes of Health (NIH) in the United States. She brings a unique combination of scientific rigour and business acumen, having completed a Global Executive MBA that has sharpened her leadership, strategy, and commercialisation capabilities across the translational research continuum.

Her work integrates human mechanistic research, clinical trials, and public health interventions, all with the aim of delivering real-world impact. She is particularly passionate about developing innovative, safe, and scalable strategies for the prevention and management of chronic diseases—strategies that can inform treatment guidelines, reduce morbidity and mortality, and lower healthcare costs. Barbora advocates for holistic, health-promoting approaches that benefit not only individuals but also society and the environment.

In recognition of her outstanding contributions to medical research and healthcare, Barbora was awarded the Order of Australia Medal in 2024. The same year, she was awarded an Honorary Fellowship from the Australasian Society of Lifestyle Medicine, reflecting her leadership and impact in the field.

At RMIT, Barbora established and directs the Centre for Health by Design, a pioneering initiative that applies design thinking and transdisciplinary collaboration—spanning design, computing, engineering, business, and health—to tackle challenges in patient care and health service delivery.

Barbora's international career includes appointments at leading institutions such as the national Institutes of Health (USA), Baker IDI and Monash University (Australia), and the University of Copenhagen and Steno Diabetes Centre (Europe). She has cultivated an active global research network, authoring over 230 scientific publications (H-index 75, 61,000+ citations on Google Scholar) and delivering more than 500 presentations at national and international forums. She has attracted over $12 million in research funding and received 20 research awards.

Her work has influenced global health policy, having been cited in seven international policy documents, including those by the World Health Organization, the World Bank, and the NIH. She has served on numerous expert panels and boards, including the Australian National Health and Medical Research Council, Diabetes Australia Research Trust, the Royal Australasian College of Physicians, and the Australian and New Zealand Obesity Society.

A committed mentor, Barbora has supervised over 100 PhD students, junior researchers, and clinicians, fostering the next generation of leaders in medical research and public health.

Describe the circumstances surrounding your first leadership position

My first opportunity to lead came after I was awarded an NHMRC Career Development Fellowship along with a few research grants at Baker IDI in Melbourne, Australia. With this support, I established a small research team—two research assistants and one student. At the time, I had no formal training in leadership or staff management. I learned on the job, often by trial and error, making mistakes, and growing through them.

After three years, I relocated to Denmark due to my husband's work. Not long after, I was recruited back to Australia by Monash University and received another NHMRC grant. Although I returned at the level of Associate Professor, the move required me to essentially rebuild my career from the ground up. I started with just one PhD student in my first year. By the end of my third year, the team had grown to include five PhD students and two research assistants. I established and led the Diabetes and Chronic Disease Prevention Laboratory within the School of Public Health and Preventive Medicine at Monash University.

To strengthen my leadership skills, I took part in several short leadership workshops offered by Monash—typically two to three days long. While they provided useful frameworks, their impact on my leadership style was limited. The real turning point came in 2020, when I enrolled in the Global Executive MBA (GEMBA) at Monash University. GEMBA significantly shaped my leadership and management capabilities, and most importantly, gave me the confidence to pursue senior leadership roles.

Soon after finishing GEMBA, I took up the role of Associate Dean at RMIT University, leading a team of 85 staff through the challenging transition from the COVID-19 pandemic back to a sense of normalcy. It was a period of rapid change, and I was proud to drive meaningful transformation within the disciplines under my leadership.

Anjali Dhulia started her medical career in the Indian Army where she served for 8 years. She completed her post-graduate training in Paediatrics from Delhi University and practised in Paediatric intensive care before migrating to Australia. She worked as a Fellow in Neonatology at the Women's and Children's Hospital in Adelaide, the Royal Women's and Royal Children's hospitals in Melbourne, and also with the Neonatal Emergency Transport Service (NETS).

She switched to a career in Medical Administration in 2008 and completed a Fellowship of the Royal Australasian College of Medical Administrators. She has worked at Northern Health and Monash Health in various medical management roles. She is currently the Chief Medical Officer at Monash Health. She has completed a Master of Public Health from Latrobe University and a Master of Applied Positive Psychology from Melbourne University.

Her professional interests and expertise include medical workforce management, healthcare safety and quality, and engagement and wellbeing of medical staff. She is passionate about workforce health and wellbeing and has led the development of Monash Health's mental health and wellbeing strategy for Monash Doctors. For this work, she was a finalist in the 2015 Leadership Victoria awards and the Strategy was judged a Silver winner at the Victorian Public Healthcare awards. In addition, she has co-led the development of Monash Health's Women in Medicine programme and the organisational Gender Action Plan 2018.

Describe the circumstances surrounding your first leadership position

My first formal leadership position was as the Director of Medical Services in a tertiary health service. My Fellowship with the Royal Australasian College of Medical Administrators included training in Medical Leadership and Management. While that did give me a theoretical grounding in leadership, it has largely been the experience on the job and life, before and after the Fellowship training, that has taught me the art of leadership. In the complex healthcare environment, one's leadership skills are constantly challenged, and it is by regular self-reflection and peer group learning that one can continue to evolve and grow as a leader.

Chris Gartside is an accomplished, dynamic, and solutions-focused senior nurse leader with expertise in public tertiary, regional, and remote healthcare settings. Chris excels in fostering clinical service excellence through strong workforce engagement and leadership. His career spans a diverse range of senior roles, from managing complex clinical operations through to leading multidisciplinary teams in challenging environments and executive leadership.

Chris's leadership is characterised by authenticity, empathy, and a deep commitment to stakeholder engagement. He is adept at navigating complex healthcare systems, driving strategic innovation and initiatives, and fostering a culture of collaboration and continuous improvement. Known for a strong commitment to evidence-based practice, data-informed decision-making, and implementing strategic improvements that enhance patient safety and care quality.

Throughout his career, Chris has been instrumental in driving organisational change, particularly in areas of clinical performance improvement. He has a proven track record in leading teams through significant transitions.

Known for his ability to build rapport and influence positive outcomes, Chris Gartside is a leader dedicated to enhancing healthcare delivery through strategic vision, clinical expertise, and a commitment to quality and safety.

Describe the circumstances surrounding your first leadership position

My first leadership position, as the Nurse Unit Manager (NUM) of an Intensive Care Unit (ICU), was thrust upon me during a period of significant leadership change and workplace culture challenges. I was working as an Emergency Department Associate Nurse Unit Manager (ANUM) and organisational Patient Flow Manager, and I was asked to transition into the role to support the team during a period of considerable change and restructure. Stepping into this role was one of the greatest leadership challenges and learning opportunities of my career. It is the environment to which I quickly learnt that I belonged and a space that I believed I could make a difference.

Christina Johnson is the Director of Monash Doctors Education; a Consultant in General and Geriatric Medicine at Monash Health; and Adjunct Clinical Professor, School of Clinical Sciences, Faculty of Medicine Nursing and Health Sciences, Monash University. She has a PhD in health professions education, and her main research interests include feedback discussions, workplace learning, and remediation.

Describe the circumstances surrounding your first leadership position

I was appointed as the Director of Monash Doctors Education, from a smaller role within the unit. I took this on as my first leadership position mid-career. Before that I had been working 2 days a week for over 10 years while my children were growing up. I had a lot to learn about leadership and management so a formal training programme course and coaching would have been useful!

Stephanie Jones graduated with an MBChB from the University of Otago, NZ, in 1996, and moved to Australia to commence Advanced Training in Infectious Diseases in 2002. After 2 years in metropolitan settings, Stephanie moved to Vietnam to complete her specialist training in local hospitals, before spending a further 5 years working in humanitarian organisations and developing countries. Returning to Australia in 2011, Stephanie took a full-time role as a General Medicine and Infectious Diseases physician at Monash Health for 4 years, with a 6- month break for maternity leave. In 2015 Stephanie took the role of Head of Unit, Dandenong Hospital, and held that role for 3 years before successfully being appointed as the Service Director of General Medicine, Monash Health.

Describe the circumstances surrounding your first leadership position

I had been working as a consultant in a General Medicine unit for 4 years and developed an interest in systems, Quality and Safety, workforce management, and improvement strategy. As my interest grew, I worked more closely alongside the Director of the unit and he encouraged me to take on delegated responsibility for some of these portfolios. When he moved into a different role, I had the knowledge and skills, as well the passion, to apply for the vacant position.

Mary Lam is a data scientist specialising in biostatistics and health informatics. She has over 15 years of experience teaching Health Informatics, Digital Health, and Co-design to both undergraduate and postgraduate students. Her expertise lies in data linkage and the analysis of large-scale health system datasets. In addition to leading her own research on health information workforce training and capacity, Mary contributes her data expertise to clinician-led research projects. She has established collaborative research relationships with colleagues in Australia and Hong Kong.

Kwang Lim is a geriatrician. He is currently the Medical Director for the Home First, Ambulatory and Complex Care Program as well as the Clinical Director for Medicine and Aged Care at Royal Melbourne Hospital. He is a Clinical Professor of Medicine for the University of Melbourne.

He has had previous roles including the Chief Medical Officer and Clinical Director of Medicine and Continuing Care at Northern Health in Melbourne. He was also the Director of Research, Northern Health.

Describe the circumstances surrounding your first leadership position

I was approached for my first leadership position to lead Aged Care at the Northern Hospital and Broadmeadows Health Service. This was not an advertised position and involved the development of the service as we had difficulty with recruiting junior staff.

Karen Livesay is the Associate Dean, Clinical Sciences at RMIT University in Melbourne, Australia. Karen is a Registered Nurse, Registered Midwife, and Certified Emergency Nurse. She has been a Nurse Academic for 16 years during which period she has led programmes, the nursing discipline, and large projects.

Karen is a leader in simulation-based learning (SBL) and a member of peak simulation bodies and has served on several advisory groups. She has worked in the design of simulated learning environments across industry and higher education. Her development and delivery in SBL is predominantly with nursing, midwifery, and paramedicine but spans 11 other health disciplines in interprofessional simulation.

Karen's research interests also centre on simulation-based learning, and she is most well known for her work with culturally and linguistically diverse simulated patients. Karen has received more than 2 million dollars in competitive research funding with her most recent grant focusing on the capacity for nurse education to address the needs of students in digital health technologies through simulation.

Describe the circumstances surrounding your first leadership position

My first recognised leadership position was as an Associate Nurse Unit Manager in an Emergency

Department. I sought out that opportunity and moved to another hospital to take up the role. I was promoted to Nurse Unit Manager 18 months later.

Erwin Loh is President-Elect of the Royal Australasian College of Medical Administrators and national Director of Medical Services at Calvary Health Care. Prior to that, he was Chief Medical Officer at Goulburn Valley Health, St Vincent's Health Australia, and Monash Health. He is a Professor at Monash University, where he leads the Clinical Leadership and Management Unit at the Monash Centre for Health Research and Implementation. He is an Honorary Clinical Professor at the Department of Medical Education, University of Melbourne. He is an Honorary Professor at Macquarie University at the Centre for Health Systems and Safety Research. He received the Distinguished Fellow Award from RACMA in 2017 for 'commitment to governance, research and publication'.

Describe the circumstances surrounding your first leadership position

My first leadership position was being a youth leader at my local church. I believe it was a calling and wasn't something I was seeking. My first professional leadership role was Deputy Chief Medical Officer at Peter MacCallum Cancer Centre, and this was a role that I applied for.

Sarah Lorentzen began her career as a physiotherapist, spending time in the public and private system in Victoria before heading to the United Kingdom to work in the NHS in a range of physiotherapy roles, and completing her clinical master's degree. On her return to Australia, Sarah transitioned from her clinical role to the world of Improvement Science, working as an Innovation and Improvement Advisor at Monash Health and eventually in the role of Director of Transformation (with a little dalliance with Digital Health in between). Sarah currently works as the Chief of Staff at Monash Health, leading a range of strategic initiatives within the Office of the Chief Executive. Outside work, Sarah teaches fitness classes, competes in master's athletics, and runs around after her two teenage children.

Describe the circumstances surrounding your first leadership position

My first significant leadership position was as School Captain. I do remember wanting the role, mostly because I thought I could do it and I'd enjoy it. It was a highly sought-after role, and I also thought my parents would be proud of me. I also have an attitude that was instilled in me by my parents and my grandmother of 'giving back' and that if you have something to give (including an opinion, a skill, a contribution), then you should give it. This doesn't necessarily hold true all the time (especially the opinion part), but it's not a bad place to start.

Mark Misquitta I am the Director of Corporate Services at Monash Health and an Adjunct Professor in the Department of Accounting at Monash University. I have spent 7 years in the healthcare industry and 20 years working in the various disciplines of finance. This has included insolvency, forensic accounting, auditing, corporate finance, strategic finance, and now procurement, supply chain, and environmental sustainability. I am also a Certified Practicing Accountant via my membership with CPA Australia.

What I have come to realise over this journey is that finances, to a certain degree, are a language that describes the behaviour and decisions of the past and can be used to try and paint a picture of the future. Though they are important, it is always practical to remember they seldom are the full or only story.

Outside of work, I love the outdoors and the sense of adventure that comes with that. I love doing multi-day camping in the remote wilderness. I also enjoy snowboarding. When I was younger, I spent a ski season working as a lift operator at a resort near Jasper, Alberta, Canada. The experience taught me how to give great customer service whilst being incredibly cold.

Describe the circumstances surrounding your first leadership position

My first leadership position was a Senior Auditor at a government agency. To get the position I had to go through a competitive process and be appointed to the role. This was a role I wanted and spent years preparing and developing for. That role taught me to let go and to get better at trusting others.

Brett Sutton AO is Director of Health & Biosecurity at CSIRO, Australia's national science agency.

He is a qualified public health physician, with extensive experience and clinical expertise in public health and communicable diseases, gained through experience in government, emergency medicine, and field-based international work.

Prior to CSIRO, he held the role of Victoria's Chief Health Officer together with the role of Victoria's Chief Human Biosecurity Officer. In this role, Professor Sutton played a leading role in guiding the public health response to COVID-19 in Victoria, including as statutory decision-maker and departmental spokesperson.

Prior to his appointment as Victorian Chief Health Officer, Professor Sutton held several senior positions within the Victorian Department of Health, including as Deputy Chief Health Officer (Communicable Disease) and within their Health Protection Branch.

Professor Sutton has specialist knowledge in tropical medicine and infectious disease, including in lower-middle-income countries and complex humanitarian environments, and has worked in various specialised health roles in Afghanistan, Ethiopia, Kenya, Timor-Leste, and Fiji.

Professor Sutton is a Fellow of the Royal Society for Public Health, a Fellow of the Australasian College of Tropical Medicine, and a Fellow of the Australasian Faculty of Public Health Medicine (AFPHM). He is also a member of the Faculty of Travel Medicine.

Describe the circumstances surrounding your first leadership position

My first leadership position is perhaps hard to define. I'd had roles of Director in Emergency Medicine and as Deputy Chief Health Officer, with a large team to manage. But if leadership positions can be defined as those when others reference your leadership approach and qualities, then I think I was 'thrust into' a leadership position during the COVID-19 pandemic. Not a position one could anticipate but clearly one with all the expectations and responsibilities of leadership!

Karin Thursky is the Director of the National Centre for Antimicrobial Stewardship (NCAS) (based at the University of Melbourne); Director of the RMH Guidance Group at the Royal Melbourne Hospital (RMH) based at the Doherty Institute; the Associate Director of Health Services Research and Implementation Science, the Professor Director of the Centre for Health Services Research in Cancer, and the Deputy Head of the Department of Infectious Diseases at the Peter MacCallum Cancer Centre. She is principal fellow in the Department of Medicine at the University of Melbourne and the Sir Peter MacCallum Department of Oncology.

Describe the circumstances surrounding your first leadership position

When I think about how I first came into a leadership position, it is really through my ability to lead innovation AND to build high-performing teams. The first example of this was at the Royal Melbourne Hospital. The success of the Guidance decision support system for antimicrobial stewardship, which was funded initially through a grant, and then adopted by hospitals across Australia, led to the formation of my own independent unit and my first director role. This was a team that grew from a handful of people to now consisting of 25 amazing clinicians, software developers, and business developers.

Rhonda Wilson, RN, CMHN, PhD, is an internationally recognised mental health nursing scientist with a research focus on mental health, digital health, and First Nations health. She is a Professor of Mental Health Nursing at RMIT and the current President of the Australian College of Mental Health Nurses. She is a Registered Nurse and Credentialed Mental Health Nurse. As a Wiradjuri descendent, Rhonda is a vigorous advocate for the promotion of cultural safety, competence, and decolonisation in research, education, and health institutions. She has extensively published in international journals, books, and conferences and frequently invited for keynote presentations. Rhonda contributed to clinical humanitarian service in the early COVID-19 vaccination campaign (2021) focused on administering vaccinations to large populations of First

Nations people in two communities: Walgett on Gomeroi Traditional land and Wyong on the Central Coast of NSW, on Darkinjung Traditional land.

Describe the circumstances surrounding your first leadership position

Early in her clinical career and working in rural Australian health services, Rhonda recalls stepping into leadership roles when local necessity demanded. She led multidisciplinary mental health, alcohol, and other drug clinical teams (community and acute inpatient) across large geographical areas that cared for diverse communities with bespoke healthcare needs. Rural clinical leadership offered dynamic experiences, autonomy, and opportunities for courageous advocacy targeting equitable outcomes for rural patients and health professionals.

Eugine Yafele Before moving to Melbourne in 2024 to lead Monash Health, Eugine was CEO at the University Hospitals Bristol and Weston NHS Foundation Trust in England. Prior to that he held senior roles at Dorset Healthcare University NHS Foundation Trust, including CEO, and in 2022 was recognised as the top CEO in the NHS by the Health Service Journal. He was appointed Visiting Professor for the College of Health, Science and Society at the University of the West of England and was a board member of the NHS Race and Health Observatory. Eugine is also an Adjunct Clinical Professor in the School of Clinical Sciences at Monash University.

Describe the circumstances surrounding your first leadership position

My first leadership role was to lead a hospital-wide quality improvement project. I was asked to do it and felt ill prepared, under qualified, and unsure albeit super excited to be given the opportunity. I knew very little about quality improvement and as it turns out about myself. I am forever grateful for what others saw in me at the time.

Contributors

Sara Baqar Department of Endocrinology, Austin Health, Melbourne, VIC, Australia

Sara Barnes Department of General Medicine, Monash Health Lung, Sleep and Allergy, Monash Health, Melbourne, VIC, Australia

Monash University, Melbourne, VIC, Australia

Don Campbell Design and Discovery Division, Northern Health, Melbourne, VIC, Australia

Ron Cheah National Centre for Antimicrobial Stewardship, Department of Infectious Diseases, Melbourne Medical School, University of Melbourne, Melbourne, VIC, Australia

RMH Guidance Group, Royal Melbourne Hospital, Melbourne, VIC, Australia

WHO Collaborating Centre for Antimicrobial Resistance, Doherty Institute, Melbourne, VIC, Australia

Allen Cheng School of Clinical Sciences, Monash University, Melbourne, VIC, Australia

Nick Coatsworth School of Regulation and Global Governance, Australian National University, Canberra, ACT, Australia

Barbora de Courten School of Health & Biomedical Sciences, STEM College, RMIT University, Melbourne, VIC, Australia

Department of General Medicine, Monash Health, Melbourne, VIC, Australia

Anjali Dhulia Monash Health, Melbourne, VIC, Australia

Chris Gartside Emergency Services and Access Division, Northern Health, Melbourne, VIC, Australia

Christina Johnson Monash Doctors Education, Monash Health, Melbourne, VIC, Australia

School of Clinical Sciences, Faculty of Medicine, Nursing and Health Sciences, Monash University, Melbourne, VIC, Australia

Stephanie Jones Department of General Medicine, Monash Health, Melbourne, VIC, Australia

Mary Lam School of Health & Biomedical Sciences, STEM College, RMIT University, Melbourne, VIC, Australia

Kwang Lim Department of Medicine, Royal Melbourne Hospital, University of Melbourne, Melbourne, VIC, Australia

Karen Livesay School of Health & Biomedical Sciences, STEM College, RMIT University, Melbourne, VIC, Australia

Erwin Loh Royal Australasian College of Medical Administrators, Melbourne, VIC, Australia

Sarah Lorentzen Monash Health, Melbourne, VIC, Australia

Mark Misquitta Strategic Finance and Governance, Monash Health, Melbourne, VIC, Australia

Department of Accounting, Monash University, Melbourne, VIC, Australia

Brett Sutton Melbourne, VIC, Australia

Karin Thursky RMH Guidance Group, Melbourne, VIC, Australia

Department of Infectious Diseases, National Centre for Antimicrobial Stewardship, Melbourne Medical School, University of Melbourne, Melbourne, VIC, Australia

WHO Collaborating Centre for Antimicrobial Resistance, Doherty Institute, Melbourne, Australia

National Centre for Infections in Cancer, Peter MacCallum Cancer Centre, Melbourne, Australia

Centre for Health Services Research in Cancer, Peter MacCallum Cancer Centre, Melbourne, Australia

Rhonda Wilson School of Health & Biomedical Sciences, STEM College, RMIT University, Melbourne, VIC, Australia

Eugine Yafele Monash Health, Melbourne, VIC, Australia

Introduction

Sara Baqar

Healthcare is an inherently complex and dynamic field, requiring leaders to not only possess technical knowledge but also the ability to inspire, support, and guide their teams through an ever-evolving landscape. As healthcare professionals, we are faced with unique challenges—rapid advancements in technology, shifting patient expectations, and the increasing demand for integrated care. These challenges require innovative leadership to navigate this landscape successfully whilst maintaining a clear vision for one's career path and purpose.

Leadership is a significant career decision that has the potential to launch you in new directions. For many, it is essential to feel in control of their career journey, charting a course that aligns with their values and goals. Career paths, while often nonlinear and full of unexpected twists, require both a strategic approach and a strong sense of self-awareness to ensure success. Without clarity, it's easy to get lost in the complexity of the healthcare environment or the wider landscape of leadership.

Understanding Leadership in Healthcare

Stepping into leadership in healthcare carries a distinctive set of responsibilities. Unlike many industries, decisions made in healthcare leadership directly influence not only organisational performance but also the lives and well-being of patients. Therefore, aspiring leaders must cultivate a diverse skill set, balancing clinical expertise with emotional intelligence, sound decision-making, and the ability to manage teams effectively under pressure. A critical component of leadership also involves mastering people management—motivating, engaging, and empowering teams for meaningful contributions.

S. Baqar (✉)
Department of Endocrinology, Austin Health, Melbourne, VIC, Australia

© The Author(s), under exclusive license to Springer Nature Singapore Pte Ltd. 2025   1
R. Junckerstorff, S. Baqar (eds.), *Leadership Pearls in Healthcare*,
https://doi.org/10.1007/978-981-96-4233-5_1

Leadership in healthcare extends beyond resolving immediate issues; it demands foresight in anticipating future challenges, fostering innovation, and creating systems that prioritise patient outcomes while safeguarding staff well-being. Furthermore, the ability to manage change is indispensable. Successful leaders navigate transitions smoothly, fostering adaptability and ensuring their teams embrace new opportunities. Effective change management not only reduces resistance but also positions organisations to innovate and thrive in a changing landscape.

This book seeks to help you understand these multifaceted aspects of healthcare leadership while supporting you in identifying and developing your personal leadership style.

Gaining Career Clarity: So Why Exactly Are You Embarking on This Journey?

Before stepping into a leadership role, it's crucial to take a step back and gain clarity on the direction of your career. Understanding yourself—your strengths, values, interests, and unique abilities—plays a key role in shaping your professional path. Leadership is not just about guiding others; it's about first knowing where you want to go and how you plan to get there.

Take time to reflect on the following questions:

- **How well do I understand my strengths and what motivates me?** Am I aware of what drives my passion and keeps me engaged in my work?
- **What kind of environment allows me to do my best work?** Do I thrive in a fast-paced setting or prefer a more thoughtful and collaborative atmosphere?
- **What types of colleagues bring out the best in me?** How do my working relationships contribute to my success and fulfillment?
- **Which organisations or sectors align with my values and ambitions?** Am I in a space that reflects my principles and long-term goals?
- **What skills do I excel at, and where do I need to grow?** How can I continuously develop to meet the demands of the evolving healthcare landscape?
- **How do I maintain my well-being while managing career growth?** What are the ways I can ensure balance between personal fulfillment and professional ambition?

Clarity in your career direction is more than just setting goals; it's about aligning your personal vision with the opportunities and environments that support your growth. Reflecting on these questions will help you build a strong foundation for your leadership journey, ensuring that every step you take is purposeful and aligned with what truly matters to you.

The Importance of Understanding Your Personality to Help You Along the Way

One of the most critical aspects of leadership is self-awareness—knowing your natural tendencies, how you approach decisions, and how you interact with others. Understanding your personality can greatly impact your effectiveness as a leader. Tools like the Myers-Briggs Type Indicator (MBTI) and Disc Assessment provide valuable insights into your behavioural preferences, offering clarity on how you engage with your team, process information, and respond to challenges [1].

These assessments are not about labelling or predicting performance but rather understanding how you instinctively operate. By exploring your personality type, you can identify the environments in which you thrive, your communication style, and the leadership approaches that come most naturally to you. This self-awareness allows you to lead authentically and helps in building diverse, complementary teams that enhance collective performance. Recognising your strengths and limitations is the foundation of strong leadership.

Discovering Your Purpose Through Ikigai

Leadership is most powerful when it is driven by a sense of purpose. The Japanese concept of *ikigai*, which translates to "reason for being," encourages individuals to find the intersection of what they love, what they are good at, what the world needs, and what they can be paid for [2]. Understanding your *ikigai* is about identifying the deeper motivations behind your work and aligning them with your career choices.

In the demanding field of healthcare, having a clear sense of purpose is essential to maintaining focus and motivation. Knowing your *ikigai* not only drives personal fulfillment but also fuels your leadership vision, helping you navigate challenges with resilience and a clear sense of direction. When your leadership is rooted in purpose, you inspire others to follow suit, creating a culture where passion and commitment are at the heart of everything you do.

Exploring your *ikigai* through reflective exercises helps clarify your long-term goals and how your work contributes to a greater good. It's not just about professional success; it's about understanding the unique value you bring to the world and how that translates into your leadership journey.

Emotional Intelligence in Leadership

As a leader, emotional intelligence (EQ) is just as important as technical expertise [3]. EQ refers to your ability to understand and manage your own emotions while recognising and influencing the emotions of others. Leaders with high emotional intelligence foster stronger relationships, resolve conflicts more effectively, and create a more positive work environment.

Daniel Goleman's framework outlines several leadership styles—visionary, coaching, affiliative, democratic, pace-setting, and commanding—each of which requires a different application of emotional intelligence [4]. For example, a visionary leader inspires through empathy and communication, while a coaching leader helps others grow by being attuned to their individual needs. Understanding these different styles and knowing when to apply them allows leaders to adapt to varying team dynamics and situations.

In healthcare, where decisions and interactions can be emotionally charged, the ability to remain composed, show empathy, and guide teams through difficult situations is invaluable. Leaders who can balance emotional intelligence with decisiveness not only drive better outcomes but also create a more supportive and engaged workforce.

Practical Wisdom in Leadership Required for Navigating Ethical Challenges

Healthcare presents leaders with unique ethical challenges that require careful consideration and balance. Decisions related to patient care, resource allocation, and organisational policy often carry ethical implications. Therefore, effective healthcare leaders will not only rely on knowledge and skills but also will need to cultivate *practical wisdom*—the ability to make prudent judgments in the face of uncertainty [5]. Practical wisdom, a concept rooted in Aristotle's *phronesis*, combines experience, values, and context. In healthcare, where decisions can have profound ethical and social implications, leaders must move beyond technical know-how and ask, "What is good for the not only the organisation, but also the patients, the staff, and society as a whole?"

Practical wisdom helps leaders weigh short-term goals against long-term societal impact. For example, it's not just about achieving established key performance indicators or profitability but considering the broader well-being of patients, communities, and staff. Leaders who embody wisdom create environments that encourage ethical decision-making and help others develop their own judgment, fostering a culture of integrity.

This book aims to provide general guidance on how to navigate these challenges with integrity, ensuring that your leadership decisions align with both ethical standards and the needs of your patients and staff.

Resilience in Leadership

Healthcare leaders often encounter significant stress and unforeseen challenges, making resilience a key trait. Resilience allows leaders to recover from setbacks, remain focused in the face of adversity, and guide their teams through tough times. As a healthcare leader, it's important to build your own resilience while also fostering a resilient team environment. The *Work-Life Balance* section will explore strategies for maintaining mental and emotional well-being under high-stress environments.

Fostering a Culture of Continuous Improvement

Great healthcare leaders not only manage teams effectively but also foster a culture of continuous improvement [6]. In this rapidly evolving field, leaders must champion innovation, encourage learning, and drive improvements in patient care and organisational processes. The *Innovation* section in this book provides insights on how to inspire your team to adopt a mindset of ongoing learning and advancement, which is critical in a field where change is constant.

Diversity and Inclusion in Leadership

In healthcare, embracing diversity and inclusion is crucial for delivering equitable care and fostering strong teams. Leaders must understand and appreciate the value of diverse perspectives and work to build inclusive teams that reflect the communities they serve. Several sections in the book, such as *Building and Sustaining Effective Teams*, will explore how to create a more inclusive work environment, promote diversity in decision-making, and ensure that all voices are heard and valued.

Leadership in Crisis Management

Effective crisis management is an essential skill for healthcare leaders. Whether dealing with a pandemic, natural disaster, or internal organisational crisis, leaders must remain calm, communicate clearly, and make decisions that protect patients and staff. This section will focus on the principles of leading through crisis, emphasising the importance of clear communication, adaptability, and decisive action in high-pressure situations.

Building a Support Network

Leadership is not a solitary journey. One of the most important resources you can cultivate as you develop your leadership skills is a strong support network. This includes mentors, peers, and colleagues who can offer guidance, feedback, and collaboration. Building meaningful professional relationships will not only help you grow but will also provide you with a community that shares your commitment to healthcare excellence. In this book, we will explore the value of networking and mentorship as part of your leadership development.

Career Transitions and Navigating Change

Whether you're transitioning into a new leadership role, changing industries, or pursuing additional growth, navigating career transitions is one of the most significant challenges any professional can face. Each transition—be it a role change, promotion, or a move to a new organisation—requires careful planning, strategic activities, and sometimes upskilling. Career clarity will enable you to make these transitions smoothly, ensuring that you're not only moving forward but doing so in alignment with your overall goals.

Along the way, you will face blockers—both real and perceived. Identifying potential constraints, such as skill gaps or emotional barriers early in the process, allows you to mitigate these challenges and move forward with confidence.

Developing a Growth Mindset

Another vital aspect of leadership in healthcare is the cultivation of a growth mindset. Leaders must be open to continuous learning and development, embracing new knowledge, technologies, and ideas that can improve patient outcomes and the workplace environment. A growth mindset encourages resilience, adaptability, and innovation—qualities that are essential in healthcare. This book will also touch on strategies for nurturing this mindset, enabling you to see challenges as opportunities for development rather than obstacles to overcome.

Conclusion

This book, *Leadership Pearls in Healthcare*, goes beyond offering strategies for leading teams—it provides a platform for personal reflection and career clarity, helping you align your current or future leadership journey with your professional and personal aspirations. By leveraging these pearls of wisdom, you can craft a career and leadership style that reflects your authentic self.

The journey to becoming a successful healthcare leader is deeply personal, requiring a balance of self-awareness, adaptability, and purpose. As you explore the scenarios and insights shared throughout this book, we encourage you to reflect not only on the leadership lessons but also on your own career trajectory. Take the time to ask the tough questions, assess your strengths, and gain clarity on what truly matters to you. In doing so, you will be well-equipped to navigate the challenges of leadership in healthcare and beyond.

References

1. Myers, I. B., & Briggs, K. C. (1995). *Gifts differing: Understanding personality type*. Davies-Black Publishing.
2. García, H., & Miralles, F. (2017). *Ikigai: The Japanese secret to a long and happy life*. Penguin Books.
3. Marston, W. M. (1928). *Emotions of normal people*. Harcourt, Brace & Company.
4. Knight, R. (2024, April). 6 common leadership styles and how to decide which to use when. *Harvard Business Review*. https://hbr.org/2024/04/6-common-leadership-styles-and-how-to-decide-which-to-use-when
5. Nonaka, I., & Takeuchi, H. (2011, May). The big idea: The wise leader. *Harvard Business Review*. https://hbr.org/2011/05/the-big-idea-the-wise-leader
6. Skills You Need. (n.d.). *Leadership skills*. SkillsYouNeed. https://www.skillsyouneed.com/leadership-skills.html

Part I
Communication

Encouraging Diverse Perspectives from the Entire Team Leads to the Best Decisions

Anjali Dhulia

Leadership Pearl

Silence and silencing is dangerous. Creating psychological safety allows team members to speak up for safety, learn from mistakes and share ideas for improvement.

Scenario

Sarah had recently joined a new organisation as the Director of the Unit. She was a relatively junior member of the Senior Medical staff and unexpectedly found herself in a leadership position where several members of the Unit were her senior by many years. Some had been her supervisors during her training. Sarah noticed that the behaviour at unit meetings was less than optimal with people speaking over one another, a few senior voices getting the majority of airtime and many members often remaining silent. Curious questions were blocked and any challenge to the status quo was met with resistance. "This is how it has always been done" was the default line. There was on-the-side banter amongst members, inappropriate remarks and aggressive behaviour that silenced any diverse perspectives.

The meeting agenda was loose with the purpose of each item not being clear and members not sure whether an item was for a decision, consultation or information sharing. At the end of the meeting, it was not clear what actions were to be taken, by whom and by when.

Sarah was concerned that the meeting was not achieving any purpose, and it seemed that the members just used it as a space to vent their frustration and criticise the establishment. Sarah sought advice from her coach about how she should

A. Dhulia (✉)
Monash Health, Melbourne, VIC, Australia

improve the meeting, raise the level of the conversation and use the time productively. Her coach gave her some simple advice:

- Clarify the purpose and outcomes of the meeting.
- Set behavioural expectations for members.
- Ensure every voice is heard.
- Run a tight agenda with clear actions following each item assigned to a designated member to report back on in an agreed timeframe.

Her coach also suggested to start with a "Leadership Reflection" where a member of the team would share reflections about Leadership with the group to help lift the level of the conversation to a higher purpose of what being a leader means. Another suggestion was to nominate a "Values Checker" at the start of the meeting who would at the end of the meeting, report back their observations on whether the meeting was conducted in line with the organisation's and profession's values. Another suggestion was to intentionally invite the silent voices to speak first and explicitly thank them for their contribution. Her coach also encouraged her to call out bad behaviour in real time and exercise her authority to ask for change if the behaviour was disruptive to the functioning of the team.

Over time, Sarah implemented all the suggested strategies. She noticed that the team was able to have more productive discussions, challenge each other's views respectfully and arrive at the best possible decisions after having a robust discussion where all perspectives were heard. The culture also spread beyond the meeting into daily interactions between team members.

Discussion

Meetings are a big part of organisational life and can be an important structure to make collective decisions, debate complex issues and share important information. Well run meetings can bring teams together to drive the work of the team forward. It is important that the Chairperson ensures adequate planning and sets the meeting up for success. The Chair must set the tone of the meeting and ensure the valuable time is used productively to progress the purpose of the meeting. They must create the psychological safety to enable members to participate, share thoughts and ideas without fear of being dismissed so that a well-considered perspective informs decision making.

According to Dr. Amy C. Edmondson, a scholar and Harvard Business School professor, "Psychological safety is a belief that one will not be punished or humiliated for speaking up with ideas, questions, concerns, or mistakes." Expanding on this concept, Timothy Clark in his book *The Four Stages of Psychological Safety*, describes four levels of psychological safety that must be present to enable fearless participation by members of a team [1]. These include:

1. **Inclusion safety** where members feel included and welcomed.
2. **Learner safety** where members feel they can ask for help without fear of embarrassment or judgement.
3. **Contributor safety** where members can offer ideas without fear of rejection.
4. **Challenger safety** where members can question the status quo and offer a counter perspective without fear of retribution.

Creating an environment of psychological safety in meetings is critical to ensuring meetings fulfil their purpose of sound decision making, progression of work and building a high performing team.

Other Gems

- *Six Thinking Hats* by Edward DeBono is a useful book that describes a technique to investigate an issue from six different perspectives in a conflict-free way. This technique can be used in meetings to make complex decisions by interrogating the issue being discussed from a range of perspectives before settling on the way forward [2].
- *The 25 Minute Meeting* by Donna McGregor outlines how to run short, sharp and purposeful meetings [3].

References

1. Clark, T. R. (2020). *The 4 stages of psychological safety*. Berrett Koehler Publishers Inc.
2. DeBono, E. (1985). *Six thinking hats: Run better meetings, make faster decisions*. Little, Brown and Company.
3. Mcgregor, D. (2018). *The 25 minute meeting: Half the time double the impact*. Wiley.

Feedback: A Team Effort

Christina Johnson

Leadership Pearl

Clinical feedback discussions—take every opportunity to coach your team to perform at their best.

Scenario

During a busy clinical shift, Dilip, an Emergency Department consultant, asks a nurse to find Ana, a new intern. Ana had been allocated a patient over an hour earlier and still had not presented the case to him. Dilip postulated several reasons as to why Ana might be taking so long.

1. Ana might have been attempting a very detailed assessment.
2. She may have been interrupted if the patient was taken for a scan.
3. Or worryingly, maybe she was just delaying so she didn't have to start seeing another patient before the end of her shift.

When Ana arrived, her case presentation was vague and hard to follow. Dilip told Ana that in the Emergency Department they liked presentations to be 'front loaded' and to start with a sentence that summarised the problem. He wondered why Ana had taken so long to do a superficial assessment, so he asked her, "Your presentation

C. Johnson (✉)
Monash Doctors Education, Monash Health, Melbourne, VIC, Australia

School of Clinical Sciences, Faculty of Medicine, Nursing and Health Sciences, Monash University, Melbourne, VIC, Australia

© The Author(s), under exclusive license to Springer Nature Singapore Pte Ltd. 2025   15
R. Junckerstorff, S. Baqar (eds.), *Leadership Pearls in Healthcare*,
https://doi.org/10.1007/978-981-96-4233-5_3

was missing some key information although you spent an hour with the patient - what were the difficulties?"

Ana explained that the patient did not speak English very well. An official interpreter was not available at the time, so she involved the patient's daughter. The daughter was extremely chatty, and rarely stopped to allow Ana to ask the next question.

Dilip smiled, "Yes, learning to interrupt politely is an important skill. I might say something like: Emergency is always busy. It's important for us to assess every patient swiftly so we can help them as quickly as possible. So please forgive me if I need to interject to keep the assessment moving."

Discussion

Feedback conversations are an important element in optimising performance. In healthcare, these interactions typically occur between a health professional taking the role of a learner and a more senior clinician taking the role of an educator. The goal is to assist a learner to understand more about the desired standard, how their current work compares with this standard, and to make plans for further development.

Below are some useful tips for conducting a feedback conversation [1, 2]:

(a) *Timeliness*—In general it's best to have a discussion soon after the event, so it's fresh in the learner's memory and the opportunity for change is maximised. For example, if feedback occurs at the end of a clinical attachment, the learner has no chance to revise their approach before they move to another setting. On the other hand, it is sensible to avoid having a feedback discussion when the learner is exhausted or distracted as it hampers reflection. For example, immediately after a medical emergency when they are overwhelmed with emotion.

(b) *Be specific*—Describing a specific example at the start of the conversation allows a learner to consider a concrete instance. This aids understanding and provides the basis for the discussion.

(c) *Actionable*—Specify practical ways to improve. Even if a goal is well understood, it is not always easy to translate this into an effective and practical strategy.

(d) *Foster a continual improvement culture*—In healthcare, initiating a feedback discussion is often viewed like venturing into 'tiger territory'! However it seems that this 'prickliness' may be a cultural phenomenon. In one study, Professor Chris Watling asked doctors who were also athletes or musicians to compare the feedback cultures between their two vocations. Participants shared how feedback was highly desired and appreciated in sport and music, in contrast to medicine [3].

Similarly, in a New Yorker article, Professor Atul Gawande describes the contrasting attitudes of healthcare workers to coaching and performance. The use of coaches to assist athletic performance was considered by healthcare workers as an obvious positive, yet they baulked at the idea that they too could benefit from a coach's insights into their professional lives [4].

(e) *Clarify the desired performance*—An expert has a clear idea of 'what constitutes high-quality work.' Often this judgment has been developed over many years, much of it based on contextualised implicit criteria. This contrasts with learners, who have a hazy picture of 'how it should be done', making it difficult for them to discern the difference between the desired performance and their own work. Unfortunately, feedback discussions often focus on 'what's wrong.' If educators spent more time demonstrating and explaining how to do a task well, this could help the learner gain greater clarity on the goal and see differences for themselves.

(f) *Working together*—The greatest benefits arise when feedback discussions are interactive and collaborative. Each participant has different pieces of the puzzle to contribute. The learner can share the reasoning behind their actions, what they are most keen to learn about, and how they prefer to learn. This information allows an educator to tailor their insights and expertise to most effectively assist a learner to advance their capabilities.

In the above scenario, Dilip described to Ana the preferred format for case presentations in the Emergency Department. This helped Ana understand the 'desired performance'. He explored what had prevented Ana from undertaking a timely and effective assessment. It turned out that all of Dilip's speculated reasons were incorrect, illustrating the importance of keeping an open mind and asking, instead of jumping to conclusions. With Ana's input, Dilip was able to tailor his advice and suggest a practical strategy that addressed the precise underlying issue.

References

1. Johnson, C. E., Keating, J. L., Watling, C. J., & Molloy, E. M. (2020). Effective feedback conversations in clinical practice. In G. Reedy, L. McKenna, S. Gough, & D. Nestel (Eds.), *Clinical education for the health professions: Theory and practice* (pp. 1–18). SpringerLink: https://link.springer.com/referenceworkentry/10.1007/978-981-13-6106-7_53-1
2. Johnson, C. E., Keating, J. L., Leech, M., et al. (2021). Development of the feedback quality instrument: A guide for health professional educators in fostering learner-centred discussions. *BMC Medical Education, 21*, 382. https://doi.org/10.1186/s12909-021-02722-8
3. Watling, C., Driessen, E., van der Vleuten, C. P., & Lingard, L. (2014). Learning culture and feedback: An international study of medical athletes and musicians. *Medical Education, 48*(7), 713–723. https://doi.org/10.1111/medu.12407
4. Personal best by Atul Gawande. (2011, September 26). *The New Yorker.* Available at https://atulgawande.com/publication/new-yorker/

The Abyss of Assumption

Sara Barnes

Leadership Pearl

Ensure you communicate regularly and clearly state what your expectations are. If you do not, people will fill the void of information with their own, potentially incorrect assumptions.

Scenario

Matthew stood in front of his team. He sighed. Why are we in this situation? Surely, I told the team six months ago about the plan and what it entailed? Why do we now have factions within the team working on different projects of their own design and making? Surely the initial discussion and communication of the plan was adequate? This was a disaster. The new space that had become available for clinical care had now been discussed with many different people, all with different valid ideas on how to proceed, but none unifying. Sylvia had organised for the space to be explored for a new acute inpatient assessment area and Anna had been working with the out patient department to use this space to enable more rapid review of recently discharged patients. How had we got here?

S. Barnes (✉)
Department of General Medicine, Department of Monash Health Lung, Sleep and Allergy, Monash Health, Melbourne, VIC, Australia

Monash University, Melbourne, VIC, Australia

Discussion

Effective communication is a key component of successful leadership [1]. Clear and concise communication is key, however as time progresses so too does the original understanding of a plan, including the impact of deviations that occur as various contingencies arise. Consistent communication and updates with regards to progress and expectations are essential [1]. By not providing regular communication opportunities, team members may fill the void of information with their own, potentially incorrect or conflicting information/ideas [2].

Although intentional inaction in leadership is a skill and tool that can be used with significant impact, it can also lead to poor communication. As a result, it must be used wisely and with insightful balance. In contrast to intentional inaction, excessive communication can unfortunately also be problematic. A constant flood of updates and emails can lead to information fatigue, potentially resulting in miscommunication secondary to incomplete attention to the communication being presented.

Within an organisation or department, a leader needs to ensure there is a clear understanding of the frequency and mode of formal communication [1]. In addition to regular communication, when a new project is commencing, further guidance on the frequency of communication and the opportunity to ask questions and provide feedback should occur [1].

The risk of poor communication is not insignificant. Poor communication affects morale, motivation, increases errors and creates disharmony. When you observe your team not performing the tasks as envisioned, it is important to step back and review how the instructions have been communicated. As in the above scenario, when people are not communicated with effectively and regularly, they will fill the void of understanding with their own assumptions.

Other Gems

- Embrace diversity as not every person can manage with a single set of instructions, nor feel comfortable with one form of communication.
- Avoid the temptation of excessive communication. This can result in information fatigue.
- As a leader, it is often not what you do but what you don't do that is important. Actively deciding not to intervene can allow your colleagues to use their initiative.
- The power of strategic inaction and the courage to stand apart from others for moral/ethical reasons can be an important lesson for developing leaders. This needs to be distinguished from leadership inertia which can cause significant harm.

References

1. Tsipurksy, G. Poor communication may be slowing down your team. *Harvard Business Review*. Online article. https://hbr.org/2023/10/poor-communication-may-be-slowing-down-your-team#:~:text=The%20absence%20of%20clear%20managerial,overall%20quality%20of%20their%20output. Accessed 28 Aug 2024.
2. Peters, L., & O'Connor, E. (2001, May–June). Informal leadership support: An often overlooked competitive advantage. *Physician Executive*, pp. 35–39.

Developing an Authentic Allyship Through Yarning with First Nations Health Professionals

Rhonda Wilson, Barbora de Courten, and Karen Livesay

Leadership Pearl

Leaders and managers who champion cultural safety and responsiveness with First Nations health professionals will improve the quality and effectiveness of dialogue [1]. By utilising Indigenous ways of knowing, being, doing and belonging, we can create a safe space for stakeholder engagement (providers and receivers of care) and quality outcomes.

Scenario

Jackie is an early career Registered Nurse and has been newly appointed to the clinical team. She identifies as an Aboriginal First Nations woman. She is the only First Nations health professional in the multidisciplinary team, and as her manager, you are keen to see her settle in with her new colleagues. This is warmly anticipated and will create a new dynamic for your team. You want to ensure that you role model allyship to support a culturally safe and responsive environment to enable Jackie to thrive in her work. This gives you the opportunity to consider your leadership role in contributing to decolonisation and in promoting Indigenous knowledge within

R. Wilson (✉) · K. Livesay
School of Health & Biomedical Sciences, STEM College, RMIT University,
Melbourne, VIC, Australia

B. de Courten
School of Health & Biomedical Sciences, STEM College, RMIT University,
Melbourne, VIC, Australia

Department of General Medicine, Monash Health, Melbourne, VIC, Australia

your healthcare setting. You have previously undertaken cultural responsiveness professional development and during that time learned about yarning techniques. You decide to introduce yarning in your regular weekly team meetings. You revise your usual agenda to signpost yarning steps and include an example of an Acknowledgement of Country statement.

Discussion

First Nations Lens

First Nations peoples' philosophy of health often relates closely to an understanding of the social/cultural determinants of health [2]. This does not always align with the dominant Westernised biomedical ways of understanding health and disease. Dialogue with First Nations health professionals can explore concepts that contribute to the decolonisation of health institutions.

Intercultural Capability

Leaders and managers are increasingly required to demonstrate their intercultural capability. The health workforce is enriched by cultural and linguistic diversity, enhancing institutional understanding of the populations they serve. First Nations health professionals continue to be underrepresented in the health workforce. First Nations nurses make up only 1.6% of the nursing workforce in Australia, which is well below population parity [3]. In the context of legislative requirements, it is a priority for leaders and managers to consider how they will recruit and retain First Nations health professionals in their teams, and to ensure culturally safe healthcare environments for all users [4]. Developing cultural responsiveness through lifelong learning is a requisite condition for leaders and managers who wish to contribute to strengthening First Nations health professionals' retention and growth in healthcare settings [5].

First Nations Leaders and Managers

First Nations leaders and managers are frequently trailblazers, without a generational strength in the health professions. Many First Nations health professionals are first-in-family to achieve leadership and management roles. They can often be described as courageous, visionary, self-sacrificial and collaborative [5]. First Nations leaders and managers are known to value a commitment to their communities and are respectful of the obligations they have within their communities [5]. First Nations leaders have been found to adopt visionary, participatory, and transformative leadership styles [5], which aligns with Indigenous knowledge that can be seen arising from (for example) yarning processes. These leaders convey a real-world relevance, facilitating intersectional understanding across diverse settings as insider champions of cultural safety and responsiveness, thus promoting their communities while staying present in their culture.

Yarning

One solution to improving cultural responsiveness in the health workplace is for leaders and managers to consider incorporating Indigenous knowledge. Recognising and adopting Indigenous ways of knowing, being, doing and belonging can help leaders and managers implement work practices that are culturally responsive [6]. Yarning is an Indigenous framework that can be applied to the leadership and management settings in a health context [7]. To implement the yarning process there are seven key steps [6]:

First, *preparation* is necessary. Participants should come to yarning with an intent to be fully and mindfully present, to actively listen to others, and to thoughtfully, kindly, and respectfully contribute to group dialogue. In the context of yarning, all participants are equal, and all should have an opportunity to speak, and to be heard. During the preparation phase, the leader or manager can adopt the role of a host, ensuring that a suitable environment is created for the gathering and that yarning participants are comfortable, feel welcomed and safe, and are introduced to each other. Hospitality such as this supports the settling into a familiarity of surroundings and navigation or wayfinding that is relevant to the workplace. Preparing an agenda with yarning terminology to signpost the process will assist participants with wayfinding across the modified approach that has been implemented.

Second, attends to *cultural protocol*, for example, an Acknowledgement of Country followed by an opportunity to explore cultural (family) and geographical/spatial connections. This stage is important as it is a leader's opportunity to intentionally position themselves to a First Nations perspective or standpoint, and (for non-Indigenous people) an opportunity to tune in to their own development as an *ally* to First Nations people. This supports the development of a culturally safe and responsive environment. Commonly, First Nations people exchange their stories of connection to culture. For example, asking: 'what is your name, where are you from, and who is your Mob?' First Nations people will seek to establish cultural connections, recognise names and locations to help establish connectedness and identify kinship lines. Mob connections to Country, culture and language groups are especially important. When this information is known, then respect can be established according to cultural protocols. Non-indigenous people live and work on Traditional Lands of First Nations people, and they can acknowledge this in a similar manner.

Third, taking time to promote *social yarning*. Sharing personal stories promotes the establishment of trust. Leadership attributes in this context include the application of emotional intelligence in both vulnerability and reflexivity. A preparedness to share something of self, while adopting an internal posture of listening to and observing self and simultaneously being in a relationship with others is necessary

[8]. Establishing connection gives rise to trust and is reinforced through social goodwill and sharing.

Fourth, *topic yarning* is only possible after the first three steps have been achieved. The scene is set, trust is established, and it is now possible to delve into deeper and respectful listening and engage in a rigorous discussion related to the main topic of the yarning (or meeting/activity). Again, reflective leadership qualities such as being observant of self, and others', feelings and actions are required. Topical yarning will likely take the bulk of the time on the agenda.

Fifth. During topic yarning it should be possible to interrogate the phenomena of interest, and with sufficient time, a *forming of new or deeper knowledge or decision-making* is possible. Leadership qualities in this stage include a commitment to promoting self-determination, holistic principles and harmonised agreed priorities, actions and plans going forward. Agreement is a desirable outcome. Achieving agreement denotes success in the implementation of a yarning process.

Sixth is the facilitation of *respectful conclusions*. This is achieved by affirming the collective learning and trust that has developed during the yarning process [9]. This is consolidated through the expression of gratitude, respect, and a coming to consensual agreement. This stage is important because it is only at this point that transformation can proceed, that is, releasing the possibility for what *can be* in the future.

The **seventh** stage is to depart the yarning/meeting committed to honouring the remembering of the yarning and to leave in the respectful pursuit of the yarns agreed course of action [10, 11].

It is important to remember that not all issues need to be resolved in one yarning session, and the process can be revisited as many times as required.

Dismantling Racism

Racism in health settings continues to the detriment of cultural safety for people within these settings, including First Nations leaders, managers, health professionals and patients [1]. Leaders and managers have a role to play in standing shoulder-to-shoulder with First Nations leaders, managers and health professionals to dismantle racism in all occurrences. It is important to reflect on and explore one's own biases, values and judgements, to include First Nations people in conversations and decisions about them, and to respectfully and courageously engage in careful bipartisan discourse [12].

Cultural Safety

Cultural safety is determined by Aboriginal and Torres Strait Islander individuals, families and communities. Culturally safe practise is the ongoing critical reflection of health practitioner knowledge, skills, attitudes, practising behaviours and power differentials in delivering safe, accessible and responsive healthcare free of racism. [13]

Cultural safety is what the person experiencing it, (or lack thereof), says it is [13], thus the only way it is possible to know if Jackie feels culturally safe with her new colleagues is to ask her directly, and then listen to and accept her assessment. It is important to recognise that cultural safety is a dynamic characteristic, and regular check-in may be necessary to gauge the strength and progress of cultural safety in the workplace.

Conclusion

Non-Indigenous leaders and managers can position themselves in allyship with First Nations leaders, managers and health professionals by aligning themselves meaningfully with an Indigenous standpoint, and cultivating emotional intelligence, empathy and change agency to champion cultural safety and responsiveness in health institutions. For all people, adopting yarning and incorporating Indigenous ways of knowing, being, doing and belonging in the workplace will support the recruitment, retention and growth of the limited First Nations health professional workforce, in turn contributing to safer health institutions and making it possible to achieve improved health outcomes aligned with Closing the Gap.

Cultural Acknowledgement

Rhonda Wilson is a mixed heritage Wiradjuri descendant. She acknowledges the Darkinjung Traditional Custodians of the land where she resides, Anaiwan Country where she was raised and her Wiradjuri Mob. She pays yindyamarra (respect) to Elders past, present, and emerging. As a matter of cultural obligation and urgency, she aims to continuously produce culturally safe scientific evidence towards strengthening and improving the health and social and emotional wellbeing outcomes of First Nations Peoples.

References

1. McGough, S., et al. (2022). There is no health without cultural safety: Why cultural safety matters. *Contemporary Nurse, 58*, 1–10.
2. Lowitja Institute. (2020). *Culture is key: Towards cultural determinants-driven health policy—Final report*. Lowitja Institute.
3. Congress of Aboriginal and Torres Strait Islander Nurses and Midwives. (2022). *'Gettin em n keepin em n growin em'. Strategies for Aboriginal and Torres Strait Islander nursing and midwifery education reform GENKE II* (p. 31). CATSINaM.
4. Nursing and Midwifery Board. (2022). *Code of conduct for nurses*. NMBA.
5. Frawley, J., et al. (2024). Navigating leadership: Knowing, being and doing. In J. Trimble, J. C. H. Tan, & A. Jiménez-Luque (Eds.), *Building bridges to inclusive leadership through the lens of cultural narratives*. Cognella Academic Publishing.

6. Mleck, S., et al. (2025). Culturally responsive health and social care practice in primary health settings for first nations people. In D. Guzys & E. Holcombe (Eds.), *An introduction to community and primary health care*. Cambridge University Press.
7. Burke, A. W., et al. (2022). Clinical yarning with aboriginal and/or Torres Strait islander peoples—A systematic scoping review of its use and impacts. *Systematic Reviews, 11*(1), 129.
8. Wyld, F., & Fredericks, B. (2015). Earth song as storywork: Reclaiming indigenous knowledges. *Journal of Australian Indigenous Issues, 18*(2), 2–12.
9. McPhail-Bell, K., et al. (2015). 'We don't tell people what to do': Ethical practice and indigenous health promotion. *Health Promotion Journal of Australia, 26*(3), 195–199.
10. Bessarab, D., & Ng'Andu, B. (2010). Yarning about yarning as a legitimate method in Indigenous research. *International Journal of Critical Indigenous Studies, 3*, 37–50.
11. D'Antoine, H., et al. (2019). A collaborative yarn on qualitative health research with aboriginal communities. *Australian Indigenous Health Bulletin, 19*(2), 2–5.
12. Geia, L., et al. (2020). A unified call to action from Australian nursing and midwifery leaders: Ensuring that black lives matter. *Contemporary Nurse, 56*, 1–12.
13. AHPRA. (2020). *The National Scheme's Aboriginal and Torres Strait Islander health and cultural safety strategy 2020–2025* (p. 28). AHPRA.

Managing Difficult Conversations

Don Campbell

Leadership Pearl

A difficult conversation is like a viva voce examination so prepare for it.

Scenario

You are the Medical Registrar on a busy General Medicine Unit in a major teaching hospital. The Nurse Unit Manager has scheduled a meeting with the patient's family after discussion with the intern. The meeting will be held at the end of the ward round immediately before the weekly multidisciplinary team meeting. The patient is a previously well, mildly confused, frail and elderly woman. She usually lives in an aged care facility and was admitted following a stroke four days earlier. She has apparently aspirated earlier this morning and is not expected to live. An Advance Care Directive is in place and specifies no escalation to Intensive Care. The family (her daughter is a nurse and her son is a lawyer), has been informed and are angry and demanding answers. You agree to attend and, as the most senior doctor present, you agree to run the meeting. You feel out of control because you don't have a good understanding of the patient and their family situation, although thankfully you are aware of the medical aspects.

At the beginning of the discussion, you find out about the patient as a person, their life's journey, and their relationship with their family. You explain what has happened and share your thoughts about the possible next steps in the patient's treatment whilst seeking family input. You express sorrow at the course of events and sympathise with the family. The family are angry and concerned about possible

D. Campbell (✉)
Division of Design and Discovery, Northern Health, Melbourne, VIC, Australia

© The Author(s), under exclusive license to Springer Nature Singapore Pte Ltd. 2025   29
R. Junckerstorff, S. Baqar (eds.), *Leadership Pearls in Healthcare*,
https://doi.org/10.1007/978-981-96-4233-5_6

deficiencies in the care process but thank you for taking the time to listen to them and explain to them what has happened. You promise to complete an incident report for the Serious Incident Oversight Advisory Committee, who will investigate further, and to report the outcomes back to the family.

Discussion

Why Are Difficult Conversations Difficult?

Difficult conversations are challenging because they combine emotional, interpersonal, and situational factors. They often involve intense emotions, fear of conflict, and the need to make decisions under conditions of uncertainty and information ambiguity.

The key to managing difficult conversations is how you manage yourself in preparing for the conversation and how you manage your emotions during the conversation. Nonviolent Communication (NVC) is a communication process aimed at fostering understanding and empathy [1]. NVC involves expressing feelings and needs without judgement and actively listening to others. Marshall Rosenberg developed the concept of NVC whilst working on racial integration in schools and organisations in the southern United States in the late 1960s. NVC encourages honest and compassionate dialogue, and focuses on observations, feelings, needs and requests to resolve conflict peacefully (see Table 1).

In applying NVC to your difficult conversations it's important to connect with what's going on emotionally inside you and to also connect with what's alive in the other person. It isn't just a mental connection, it's an empathic connection. Lastly, NVC involves honest expression of these observations, feelings, needs and requests.

The principal exhortation is to know yourself. How do you talk to yourself? How do you recognise and respond to tension? Do you recognise the time course of your own emotional responses when you're faced with tension? Think about your thoughts when you are tense compared with when you feel quiet and calm. Is your self-talk different?

A difficult conversation is rather like an oral (viva-voce) examination so prepare for it.

Table 1 The key components of nonviolent communication

Observations	Focus on the facts rather than their meaning/significance.
Feelings	Emotions/sensations rather than thought or story content.
Needs	Refers to universal human needs. They include sustenance and safety, love and understanding, creativity, belonging, autonomy and a connection with a sense of meaning in one's life.
Requests	Different from demands. It's important to be open to hearing the word "no", without this triggering an attempt to force the matter to a conclusion.

Examples include:

- Family meetings to discuss patient management.
- Referring a patient for takeover of care.
- Talking with an underperforming junior doctor.
- Raising a topic with your head of department.

Conversations are a performative art. They consist of words plus actions. The conversation comprises discrete elements: a beginning, a middle and an end.

Having a difficult conversation is a set play. There are two (or more) actors on the stage, and you can control (only) one of them.

My Checklist Before/During/After a Difficult Conversation

Before the Conversation

1. Who called the meeting? Why is this conversation happening?
2. What do you want to get out of the conversation?
3. What does the other party hope to get out of the conversation?
4. What are the possible consequences of all possible outcomes of the meeting?
5. Mentally prepare yourself:
   - Make sure you are present in the moment.
   - Leave your ego at the door.
   - Behave as though you have all the time in the world.
   - Acknowledge your own emotions.

The Conversation itself

1. Show respect: never, <u>ever</u> interrupt the other person's opening statement.
2. Stay calm
3. Listen actively to empathise.
4. Body language: your biggest asset is your smile. Make your eyes and teeth work for you. Have your eyes at the same level as the person you are speaking to.
5. Clarify and paraphrase what you heard the other person say.
6. Express yourself clearly: be specific about the issue rather than making generalisations.
7. Seek to find common ground and trust whilst establishing boundaries to the conversation.
8. Focus on solutions but stay open-minded.
9. Use silence effectively to manage tension and achieve the desired outcome(s).
10. Know when it's time to seek help and stop the conversation.

After the Conversation

1. Document the conversation.
2. Debrief with colleagues in a safe space.
3. Reflect on your practice and learn from the experience.
4. Follow-up if necessary.

Difficult Conversations in Healthcare Settings

In medical practice, we often encounter difficult conversations that require sensitivity and the skills of effective communication, empathy and active listening. Each difficult conversation requires a tailored and compassionate approach. Some common examples include breaking bad news, end-of-life discussions, treatment decision-making, conflict with a patient or their family and discussing next steps after either an adverse event or a medical error.

Difficult Conversations with Patients

In managing difficult conversations with patients and families, stay calm, listen actively, empathise, use open-ended questions to clarify concerns and maintain a professional stance. Set clear boundaries to the conversation, involve other team members as appropriate and try to offer realistic options for discussion where they exist.

Learning to manage difficult conversations with patients is a lifelong learning process. You will learn to prioritise patient well-being whilst maintaining professional boundaries. Remember, tailoring your approach to the individual patient and their family is crucial. A flexible open mindset, empathy and a commitment to effective communication will contribute to positive outcomes in challenging interactions.

Other Gems

- An aphorism that you might find helpful:

  Every patient is an angel, a messenger sent by God to teach me a lesson.

- Your job is to work out what that lesson is and to stay humble in the process.

Reference

1. Marshall, R. (2005). *Nonviolent communication: A language of life*. PuddleDancer Press.

Part II

Building and Sustaining Effective Teams

Healthcare Is a Team Sport

Erwin Loh

Leadership Pearl

Healthcare is a team sport. In a team, you need to learn when to lead and when to follow, and when to use team members according to their strengths and weaknesses.

Scenario

You are chair of the hospital's antimicrobial stewardship working group, made up of unit heads from infectious diseases, general medicine, general surgery and orthopaedics. The National Quality Commission has released new post-operative antibiotic guidelines. The heads of the different specialty units refuse to agree on a consensus pathway for your hospital. You spend time building trust between the members of the working group and explaining the principles of effective followership and teamwork. Over time, the working group is able to come together effectively to agree on a set of antibiotic guidelines for the hospital.

Discussion

Doctors and other clinicians are all taught to be leaders of healthcare teams. However, there are two sides to leadership. Aristotle once stated that "He who cannot be a good follower cannot be a good leader" [1]. There are four types of followers [2].

E. Loh (✉)
Royal Australasian College of Medical Administrators, Melbourne, VIC, Australia

(a) "Sheep" followers, who are uncritical and passive, lacking in initiative.
(b) "Yes people", who say yes without questioning.
(c) "Alienated" followers, who are critical and independent in their thinking, but who are disengaged.
(d) "Effective followers" are team members who are highly independent and critical, as well as active and engaged.

Junior doctors tend to fall into categories (a) and (b) as they lack content knowledge, engagement and empowerment. Alienated followers are often cynical and some senior doctors may fall into this category.

It is essential that we teach clinicians to be effective followers as well as leaders. The health system is no longer a predictable and stable environment, but rather a "VUCA" (volatile, uncertain, complex, ambiguous) environment [3]. As such, doctors and other clinicians need to adopt "dynamic followership", where they take on the role of leader or follower depending on the talents of team members and the context of the situation [4].

Members of a healthcare team should also adopt five behaviours that lead to an effective team [5].

 (i) Team members need to learn to trust one another and be genuinely transparent and honest with each other in a safe environment.
 (ii) They need to be able to engage in debate and conflict constructively around ideas.
(iii) They need to be able to offer different opinions and to commit to decisions together.
(iv) They need to hold each other accountable for decisions made together.
 (v) And lastly, they need to focus on achieving collective results as a team.

In this manner, you can turn a disparate group of individuals with diverse opinions and talents into a cohesive team that is able to lead and follow each other to achieve the optimum results for you and your organisation.

Other Gems

- Remember that as a leader you are there to serve your followers and support them so that they can serve others—the essence of servant leadership. This way, followers become more effective in their followership.
- A practical expression of followership is managing up to your manager, which is the ability to communicate effectively with your line manager so that you can achieve results for you, your manager and the organisation.
- As the saying goes, there is no "I" in TEAM, and TEAM stands for "Together Everyone Achieves More." As Aristotle also stated: "The whole is greater than the sum of its parts."

References

1. Goodreads [Internet] (2024, April 22). *San Francisco (US): Goodreads; c2024.* Aristotle quote; [cited 2024 Apr 24]. Available from: https://www.goodreads.com/quotes/361140-he-who-cannot-be-a-good-follower-cannot-be-a
2. Kelly, R. (1988, November). In praise of followers. *Harvard Business Review.*
3. Bennis, W., & Nanus, B. (1985). *Leaders: Strategies for taking charge.* Harper & Row.
4. Tobin, D. W. (2023). Recognizing and illuminating the leadership/followership balance in the VUCA environment. In S. K. Dhiman, J. S. Marques, J. Schmieder-Ramirez, & P. G. Malakya (Eds.), *Handbook of global leadership and followership.* Springer.
5. Lencioni, P. M. (2024). *The five dysfunctions of a team.* Jossey-Bass.

Support Women: Kindness, Flexibility and Sponsorship

Karin Thursky and Ron Cheah

Leadership Pearl

Tailor your approach to support women wherever possible.

Scenario

The Australian workforce continues to grapple with the issue of inequity and exclusion. This is no different in the healthcare setting, and despite recent efforts to address some of these longstanding issues, mentorship and sponsorship

K. Thursky (✉)
Royal Melbourne Hospital Guidance Group, Melbourne, VIC, Australia

National Centre for Antimicrobial Stewardship, Department of Infectious Diseases, Melbourne Medical School, University of Melbourne, Melbourne, VIC, Australia

WHO Collaborating Centre for Antimicrobial Resistance, Doherty Institute, Melbourne, VIC, Australia

National Centre for Infections in Cancer, Peter MacCallum Cancer Centre, Melbourne, Australia

Centre for Health Services Research in Cancer, Peter MacCallum Cancer Centre, Melbourne, Australia

R. Cheah
Royal Melbourne Hospital Guidance Group, Melbourne, VIC, Australia

National Centre for Antimicrobial Stewardship, Department of Infectious Diseases, Melbourne Medical School, University of Melbourne, Melbourne, VIC, Australia

WHO Collaborating Centre for Antimicrobial Resistance, Doherty Institute, Melbourne, VIC, Australia

© The Author(s), under exclusive license to Springer Nature Singapore Pte Ltd. 2025
R. Junckerstorff, S. Baqar (eds.), *Leadership Pearls in Healthcare*,
https://doi.org/10.1007/978-981-96-4233-5_8

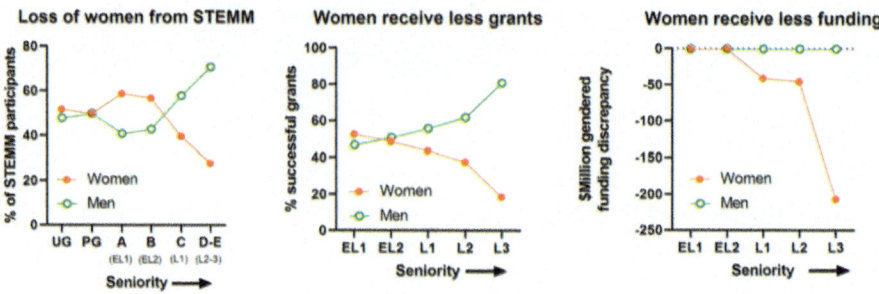

Fig. 1 As seniority increases, women receive less grants and funding, aligning with the loss of women in STEMM (Science, Technology, Engineering, Mathematics and Medicine). [2]

opportunities are still unfairly skewed. Published data on gender disparity in higher academic positions also supports this depressing narrative. Despite an almost equal representation among early career researchers, this disparity increases with seniority [1]. Recent Australian media coverage of funding for a newly created Investigator Grants Scheme revealed that at the most senior academic level, only 21% of awardees were women, equating to an additional $66 million allocated to support their senior male counterparts [2]. The net outcome of this is unsurprisingly a loss of senior women leaders [2] (see Fig. 1). Furthermore, typical academic pathways such as full-time PhDs are simply not feasible in female predominant careers such as nursing and allied health. The challenges of child rearing, and the departures from the workforce leads to further reduced productivity and slower career progression [3].

Discussion

In my leadership roles and based on my lived experience as a female clinician researcher, I am acutely aware of the inequity in opportunities in research particularly for clinician and non-clinician researchers. For example, medical researchers tend to receive more opportunities than non-medical researchers and academics often have more opportunities than non-academic clinicians. The research funding environment is incredibly tough and embarking on a research career leads to a lot of anxiety. This is acutely felt, especially by female researchers.

I have supervised many female PhDs from medical, nursing and pharmacy backgrounds. During our discussions about their research plans, I prioritise spending an equal amount of time ensuring that they are able to manage research, clinical and caregiving roles. This includes being very supportive of their maternity leave, supporting their research projects during their absence and encouraging them to return part-time particularly if they are struggling with time. I try to actively sponsor [4] them—this means providing new opportunities, connecting them with key leaders in the field, supporting conference presentations and additional publications beyond their own thesis, including providing them with last author opportunities.

Kindness and understanding regarding the personal circumstances and responsibilities of staff is equally essential. Implementing flexible policies for work schedules, remote work options, and adequate sick and caregiving leave are necessary. These are important to ensure a motivated workforce. Although very useful for flexibility, hybrid work models do require additional effort to keep staff motivated. It is important to set expectations early about which days or for which meetings staff are expected to come into the office.

Other Gems

- Be kind and generous in your leadership.
- Create opportunities for mentorship and pathways for female leadership.

References

1. Llorens, A., Tzovara, A., Bellier, L., Bhaya-Grossman, I., Bidet-Caulet, A., Chang, W. K., Cross, Z. R., Dominguez-Faus, R., Flinker, A., Fonken, Y., & Gorenstein, M. A. (2021). Gender bias in academia: A lifetime problem that needs solutions. *Neuron, 109*(13), 2047–2074.
2. Torres, A. J., Barbosa-Silva, L., Oliveira-Silva, L. C., Miziara, O. P., Guahy, U. C., Fisher, A. N., & Ryan, M. K. (2024, March). The impact of motherhood on women's career progression: A scoping review of evidence-based interventions. *Behavioral Sciences., 14*(4), 275.
3. Women's Agenda. *We need to address gender bias in medical research peer review.* [Internet]. Available from: https://womensagenda.com.au/latest/the-gender-bias-in-peer-review/
4. Baumgarten, M. (2016, August). The key role of sponsorship. *Stanford University, 1*, 2021.

Clinical Leaders Can Become Powerful Therapeutic Agents by Being Authentic and Vulnerable

Karen Livesay and Barbora de Courten

Leadership Pearl

Authentic leaders who show vulnerability create trust. Trust aids conversations between healthcare providers and benefits client safety. When health professionals feel safe to contribute, multidisciplinary relationships enable information gathering to achieve deeper insights. Through curiosity and improved relationships, better health outcomes can be achieved.

Scenario

When Jo took over as the Nurse Unit Manager (NUM) on Ward 6 East, she could see the influence on quality improvement of the previous manager in contradictory ways. Messaging on notice boards reflected the hospital's values of honesty and integrity. Speaking up and supporting a "no blame" culture was highlighted. Yet, staff behaviour reflected "naming and shaming" of colleagues and peers in written incident reports, entries in patient notes and messages shared at handover.

Jo understood she needed to set a new tone as part of developing an ethical culture. Jo needed to build credibility in openness and normalising mistakes for

K. Livesay
School of Health & Biomedical Sciences, STEM College, RMIT University, Melbourne, VIC, Australia

B. de Courten (✉)
School of Health & Biomedical Sciences, STEM College, RMIT University, Melbourne, VIC, Australia

Department of General Medicine, Monash Health, Melbourne, VIC, Australia

learning. Working with the senior staff on the ward, Jo exampled managing errors. On every occasion an error was reported, Jo shared a mistake she had previously made and what she had learned. While some foreseeable and careless mistakes were frustrating, Jo owned her feelings and shared those too.

> I hate it when I am careless, rushing and then having to deal with the fallout of doing something dumb, feels ten times worse doesn't it?

Even trying to understand misplaced beliefs was part of Jo's vision to create a culture of safety and learning.

Patient Eric was re-admitted to the ward with non-healing leg ulcers. His ulcers were contaminated with animal hair, infected and were potentially limb threatening. Eric described removing the dressings himself, a decision many of the nursing staff could not understand. Some suggested that Eric had chosen to not be compliant with the recommended management of his ulcers. At this point Jo recounted a situation where she had previously described a patient as 'non-compliant' but had come to realise that this term implied the patient was at fault. Jo's admission of vulnerability and authenticity empowered the team to question Eric's 'non-compliance.' The nursing students worked with Eric to understand why he had removed the dressings and allowed the wound to become contaminated.

Eric explained that he could not afford new dressings. He thought open wounds would be better than wounds covered with contaminated dressings. With the assistance of a social worker and community nursing assistance, a plan for Eric's ongoing wound care and dressings was established.

Discussion

The Role of Error in Learning

Errors are frequently cast as events to be avoided in healthcare. The seminal paper reporting the extent of error in healthcare "To err is human: building a safer health system" [1] is acknowledged as shifting the focus of errors from accountability to system improvement and in doing so, actively seeking insight from errors. Nonetheless, error is often associated with negative self-perception and a breach of trust [2]. When a fear of professional reprisal for mistakes prevails, the potential to engage in open discussion and forums aimed at learning, systems improvement or individual reflection, are limited. Issuing new guidelines, single points of training and sending out alerts are considered weak change strategies [3]. The World Health Organisation (WHO) recognises that reporting risk needs to be supported by a culture of curiosity [3]. In the above scenario, Jo models her own learning and fallibility. Contextual factors are a vital consideration in quality improvement initiatives and leadership is considered a key element [4].

Normalising Learning from Error Through Psychological Safety

The WHO recommends that clinicians are engaged by local leaders to reduce cultural resistance to change for successful safety risk reduction [3]. It is through the support of the social systems in healthcare that culture is influenced. Psychological safety involves individuals being comfortable to speak, question, share thoughts and mistakes without fear, shame, or ridicule [5]. According to Torralda et al., leaders can promote psychological safety by inviting participation and responding supportively and in doing so, counterbalance the implicit socialisation of negative norms [5]. O'Donovan and Mcauliffe's systematic review of psychological safety in healthcare reported enablers for psychological safety. Out of the 7 team level enablers identified, 4 were related to the behaviour of leaders: behavioural identity, change-oriented leadership, familiarity with colleagues, and leader support [6].

Culture of Learning Development

Learning from failure is encouraged by psychological safety and developed within a group for the purpose of sharing knowledge [7]. Leaders can build a psychologically safe culture that will enable staff to speak up, encourage team creativity, team learning and enhance performance. This is associated with leader behaviours such as inviting participation and supporting conversation, demonstrating transparency, and resolving conflict [7]. When Jo commenced her role as NUM on ward 6 East, errors were being reported however the reporting process highlighted liability and blame. In reality, under-reporting of errors remains significant, and the extent is dependent on whether culture is focussed on learning or accountability [3]. Jo normalised reflection on past action as a strategy to inform future action and an openness to mistakes to influence culture.

Conclusion

Feeling safe to contribute to discussions, raise concerns, admit mistakes is encouraged through the behaviour of clinical leaders. Staff learn to respond according to their perception of safety and consequences. Open dialogue facilitates reciprocity where psychological safety is genuinely present.

References

1. Kohn, L. T., Corrigan, J. M., & Donaldson, M. S. (Eds.). (2000). *To err is human: Building a safer health system*. Committee on Quality of Health Care in America, Institute of Medicine, National Academy Press. (unit.no). https://pubmed.ncbi.nlm.nih.gov/25077248/
2. Rodziewicz, T. L., & Hipskind, J. E. (2020). Medical error prevention. In *StatPearls*. StatPearls Publishing.

3. World Health Organization. (2020). *Patient safety incident reporting and learning systems: technical report and guidance.* 9789240010338-eng.pdf (who.int) https://www.who.int/publications/i/item/9789240010338
4. Coles, E., Anderson, J., Maxwell, M., Harris, F. M., Gray, N. M., Milner, G., & MacGillivray, S. (2020). The influence of contextual factors on healthcare quality improvement initiatives: A realist review. *Systematic Reviews, 9,* 1–22.
5. Torralba, K. D., Jose, D., & Byrne, J. (2020). Psychological safety, the hidden curriculum, and ambiguity in medicine. *Clinical Rheumatology, 39,* 667–671.
6. O'Donovan, R., & Mcauliffe, E. (2020). A systematic review of factors that enable psychological safety in healthcare teams. *International Journal for Quality in Health Care, 32*(4), 240–250.
7. Edmondson, A. C., & Bransby, D. P. (2023). Psychological safety comes of age: Observed themes in an established literature. *Annual Review of Organizational Psychology and Organizational Behavior, 10*(1), 55–78.

Holistic Support for an Underperforming Employee

Barbora de Courten, Karen Livesay, and Rhonda Wilson

Leadership Pearl

Supporting an underperforming employee needs to be holistic and foster long-term support and development. It starts with active listening to understand the employee's perspective of the issues. Then with the employee's perspective, the leader can share constructive feedback. Through supportive leadership, the leader can provide targeted training to address skill gaps, set clear expectations by co-designing SMART goals and finally, exercise accountability by regularly monitoring progress.

Scenario

Dr. NC is an international medical graduate and an endocrinology trainee pursuing a PhD in clinical research at one of Melbourne's universities. As a part of her PhD, NC is running a clinical trial with other PhD students who work in the same team and share some of the data collection and research papers from the same trial. Their supervisor, A/Prof JW is a mid-career scientist aiming for promotion in the next couple of years and hence is driven to meet all of her key research performance indicators. JW leads a team of five, including two PhD students, who have a

B. de Courten (✉)
School of Health & Biomedical Sciences, STEM College, RMIT University, Melbourne, VIC, Australia

Department of General Medicine, Monash Health, Melbourne, VIC, Australia

K. Livesay · R. Wilson
School of Health & Biomedical Sciences, STEM College, RMIT University, Melbourne, VIC, Australia

© The Author(s), under exclusive license to Springer Nature Singapore Pte Ltd. 2025   47
R. Junckerstorff, S. Baqar (eds.), *Leadership Pearls in Healthcare*,
https://doi.org/10.1007/978-981-96-4233-5_10

biomedical background hence cannot contribute to clinical trial activities requiring a physician. While A/Prof JW strives to distribute work evenly, NC, being the only clinician, handles most clinical tasks for the trial. Additionally, NC is required to perform data analysis and write research papers for her PhD. Despite agreed timelines, NC frequently misses deadlines, requesting extensions and sharing her rationales for not completing her work at the weekly team meetings. This pattern frustrates A/Prof JW, as it disrupts team dynamics and impacts other students' timelines. A/Prof JW has communicated the broader impact of these delays to NC and even allowed NC to set her own deadlines, but nothing has changed.

Discussion

How does a leader provide holistic support for under-performing employees?

Constructive Feedback and Active Listening

The first step in supporting NC involves active listening with giving full attention to NC, acknowledging her concerns, and responding thoughtfully. JW should listen to NC's explanations and ask clarifying questions to fully understand her situation. This can help build trust and support NC. JW should create a safe space for NC to express her challenges openly [1]. The next step is providing constructive feedback. Constructive feedback should be specific, focusing on behaviours and outcomes, rather than personal or family attributes. For example, JW could say, "I've noticed that the deadline for submitting your research paper we agreed was last Monday has not been achieved. Can you tell me from your perspective why that has occurred? Can we discuss how I can help you to meet these deadlines? What do you need from me?" This approach opens the door for NC to share her challenges without feeling judged [1].

Identifying Root Causes

Understanding the root causes of NC's under-performance is crucial. These may include:

- **Time Management Issues:** Balancing clinical tasks and research can be challenging. NC might struggle to allocate sufficient time to each task, leading to missed deadlines. She might also feel pressured by JW or the team to deliver tasks faster than she is able to.
- **Skill Gaps:** Potential gaps in data analysis, language training or academic writing skills might hinder NC's ability to complete tasks efficiently.

By identifying these root causes, JW can tailor support to address NC's specific needs [2].

Supportive Leadership and Targeted Training

JW should adopt a supportive leadership approach, providing targeted training to address any skill gaps. This could involve:

- **Professional development:** Providing an opportunity to attend workshops on time management, data analysis, and academic writing could help NC develop the necessary skills to perform her tasks more effectively.
- **Mentorship:** Pairing NC with a mentor who is not her supervisor and has no conflict of interest. A mentor can offer practical advice, share experiences, and help NC navigate her challenges.
- **Access to employee services:** JW may suggest for NC to access an Employee Assistance Program.

Supportive leadership also involves showing empathy and understanding. JW should acknowledge the challenges NC faces and offer encouragement and reassurance.

Setting Clear Expectations with SMART Goals

JW and NC should co-design SMART goals (Specific, Measurable, Achievable, Relevant, Time-bound) to set clear expectations [3]. This collaborative approach ensures that NC understands her responsibilities and has a realistic timeline to achieve them. For example, instead of a vague goal like "improve timeliness of research paper submission," a SMART goal would be "submit the first draft of the research paper on the clinical trial by October 15th, with weekly progress check-ins." This goal is specific, measurable, achievable, relevant, and time-bound, providing clear direction and accountability.

Exercising Accountability

Regularly monitoring progress is essential for ensuring accountability. JW should schedule frequent check-ins with NC to review her progress, address any emerging issues, and adjust goals as needed. This ongoing support should help NC to stay on track and feel supported. During these check-ins, JW should provide constructive feedback on NC's progress, celebrate small wins, and discuss any obstacles. This continuous engagement reinforces the importance of meeting deadlines and maintaining high performance.

References

1. Groysberg, B., & Slind, M. (2012). Leadership is a conversation. *Harvard Business Review, 90*(6), 76–84.
2. Schwartz, T. (2022). To coach leaders, ask the right questions. *Harvard Business Review*, 144.
3. https://www.forbes.com/advisor/business/smart-goals/

Avoid Micromanagement

Kwang Lim

Leadership Pearl

Set the vision and parameters and trust your staff to implement and manage.

> If you treat an individual as he is, he will remain how he is. But if you treat him as if he were what he ought to be and could be, he will become what he ought to be and could be. (Johann Wolfgang von Goethe)

Scenario

A community hospital was faced with the prospect of developing a new cardiology service. This involved hiring a whole department, including a Director of Cardiology, setting up an interventional service (this is a 24-hour, time-critical service that is on call to take patients having heart attacks to a catheter lab to place a stent in an artery in the heart). The Head of the Division of Medicine was not a cardiologist, and as a result the processes, guidelines and protocols were all somewhat foreign to them. Regardless, there were certain outcome parameters that could be established; time taken for the patient to reach the catheter lab, success of the procedure, complications, and the number of procedures that would need to be done in and out of hours. The Department also had a broader vision; to serve the community by providing a full suite of quality cardiology services in a timely manner.

The new Director of Cardiology was also completely new to the role and the hospital but had an immense work ethic and was motivated to succeed. He also had

K. Lim (✉)
Royal Melbourne Hospital, Department of Medicine, University of Melbourne, Melbourne, VIC, Australia

© The Author(s), under exclusive license to Springer Nature Singapore Pte Ltd. 2025   51
R. Junckerstorff, S. Baqar (eds.), *Leadership Pearls in Healthcare*,
https://doi.org/10.1007/978-981-96-4233-5_11

a department of staff who shared the same vision. The department developed into a successful unit that has since quadrupled in size.

Discussion

There are many leaders who micromanage, in effect disempowering their co-workers and colleagues. In clinical settings, decisions need to be made daily, mostly with minimal consequences, provided one has the confidence, support, and availability of a leader to ask if problems arise. Often there is more than one way to solve a problem. The proposed solution may not be how the team leader/manager would approach the problem, but results in a very similar outcome. It is important to set clear goals and expectations and provide the necessary resources for an employee to succeed. There needs to be clear communication regarding which decisions can be made independently and those that require further consultation with the team.

Studies have shown that micromanagement, a situation where managers feel the need to control aspects of their employees' work and decision-making to an extreme degree, has a detrimental effect on employees. DeCaro and colleagues demonstrated that employees who feel that they are being micromanaged perform at a much lower level [1].

Amabile and Kramer in *The Progress Principle* talk about the fact that to have intrinsic motivation, people need to have some say in their own work [2]. This in turn improves creativity. A key aspect of autonomy is feeling that one's decisions will hold. If these decisions are overridden by management, people quickly lose motivation to make any decisions.

As stated by Stephen Covey, "If you can hire people whose passion intersects with the job, they won't require any supervision at all. They will manage themselves better than anyone could ever manage them. Their fire comes from within, not from without" [3].

Other Gems

- Set clear goals and a vision.
- Support staff with adequate resources and be available to assist.
- Surround staff with a strong team.

References

1. DeCaro, M. S., Thomas, R. D., Albert, N. B., & Beilock, S. L. (2011). Choking under pressure: Multiple routes to skill failure. *Journal of Experimental Psychology: General, 140*(3), 390–406. https://doi.org/10.1037/a0023466

2. Van der Meer, Han, and Jan Buijs. (June 2012). "The Progress Principle–By Teresa Amabile and Steven Kramer." *Creativity and Innovation Management 21*(2), 242–243. https://doi.org/10.1111/j.1467-8691.2012.00645.x.
3. Covey, S. R. (2004). *The 7 habits of highly effective people: Restoring the character ethic.* Free Press.

Hold the Mop

Nick Coatsworth

Leadership Pearl

The principle of "Hold the Mop" is closely aligned with servant leadership but adds a layer of practical symbolism and frontline credibility.

Scenario

This concept emerged from my experience in Tacloban City during the Typhoon Haiyan disaster response, where our team was running a surgical field hospital.

During a torrential downpour, the entire field hospital was flooded. Without a second thought, I picked up a mop and started helping to clean up the flooded tents. This action, though simple, held significant symbolic value and illustrated an important aspect of leadership.

Discussion

In a crisis, a leader has many pressing responsibilities. However, picking up the mop and helping to clean was an act of solidarity significant in maintaining morale. The small acts demonstrate effective leadership by being part of the team and not just directing from above. It shows that no task is beneath the leader and that the leader is willing to do whatever it takes to support the team and the mission. It speaks to the principle of frontline credibility.

N. Coatsworth (✉)
School of Regulation and Global Governance, Australian National University,
Canberra, ACT, Australia

© The Author(s), under exclusive license to Springer Nature Singapore Pte Ltd. 2025   55
R. Junckerstorff, S. Baqar (eds.), *Leadership Pearls in Healthcare*,
https://doi.org/10.1007/978-981-96-4233-5_12

In healthcare, maintaining frontline credibility is crucial. This may involve making difficult choices about how much time to spend in clinical practice versus administrative duties. As one progresses in their career, there may come a point where it is no longer feasible to balance both. However, for as long as possible, maintaining a presence on the frontline enhances leadership skills and builds trust and respect among colleagues. It also ensures that leaders remain connected to the realities of clinical practice and the challenges faced by frontline staff.

The 'Hold the Mop' principle extends beyond crisis situations. In day-to-day clinical practice, it means being willing to perform any task if it benefits the team and/or your patients. It means showing up, being present, and demonstrating through actions that you are committed to the collective effort. This principle helps to break down hierarchical barriers and fosters a culture of mutual respect and collaboration.

For example, as Executive Director of Medical Services at Canberra Health Services, I made it a point to be actively involved in the day-to-day operations. This included participating in rounds, attending multidisciplinary team meetings, and being available to address any issues that arose. By being present and engaged, I was able to build strong relationships with my colleagues and ensure that we worked together effectively to provide the best possible care for our patients.

The 'Hold the Mop' principle is as much about how a leader behaves around their team as it is about frontline credibility. It is best described as doing the simple things and doing them regularly. Attending to smaller tasks needn't take up enormous chunks of the day. Remembering birthdays of staff in your immediate team is a technique that a mentor of mine used to show their team that they were valued. Pick one or two simple things that differentiate you as a leader. Whether it's remembering a birthday, making your staff a cup of tea when the going gets tough, or cleaning up after the unexpected, people will remember you by it.

Other Gems

- Spend time on the frontline, even if that means de-prioritising other tasks in the working week.
- To remain credible as a clinical leader, take the challenge of balancing ongoing clinical practice with senior leadership roles.

It's Always Been a Matter of Trust

Sarah Lorentzen

Leadership Pearl

Trust is the foundation of most successful organisations and indeed the foundation of most successful relationships. To trust and be trusted is the single most important aspect of successful leadership.

Scenario

I was in charge of organising a big event for the top 100 leaders in my organisation. It was extremely important that this event went well, and I felt an overwhelming sense of responsibility for it. One of many decisions I made about this event was the catering. I carefully chose things from the catering menu to manage a broad range of dietary preferences, but I also chose things that I thought people would enjoy eating. When I went to confirm all the details with my boss, he put big red lines through all my catering choices and instead selected what I'd classified as the 'boring' stuff. Nothing with relish (potential for slopping), no noodles (again, slopping), no pastries (think of the crumbs!). Even though this was not a life and death situation, and really made little material difference to the event, it made me feel not only that I wasn't trusted, but my boss didn't even trust his people not to slop relish down their clothing. It made me think, if he doesn't trust us with relish, what does he trust us with?

S. Lorentzen (✉)
Monash Health, Melbourne, VIC, Australia

Discussion

We think of trust as a precious commodity, however it is the basis for almost all of civilisation. We hand over our hard-earned money for goods and services because we trust that we will get something of value in return. We open our hearts to our nearest and dearest because we trust our hearts won't be trampled on.

Trust is defined as a firm belief in the reliability, truth, or ability of someone or something. It certainly can be thought of as something that relationships are based on, but according to the Harvard Business Review, it is also the foundation of most successful organisations [1].

According to one study, people working at high-trust companies report 74% less stress, 106% more energy at work, 50% higher productivity, 13% fewer sick days, 76% more engagement, 29% more satisfaction with their whole lives (not just their work lives) and 40% less burnout than people at low-trust companies [2].

And it all starts with leadership. Leaders have a crucial role to play in both trusting their people and being trusted. So it goes both ways.

It starts with establishing an environment where people feel safe to express their views, where they feel their contribution is valued and they can take some calculated risks without significant negative consequence. Leaders need to be authentic, transparent and set clear expectations of their people.

Frances Frei and Anne Morriss [1] believe that trust has three core drivers: authenticity, logic and empathy. When people believe they are interacting with the 'real' person (authenticity), they tend to trust them. When they have faith in someone's judgement and competence (logic) they tend to trust them. When they feel that the person they are dealing with actually cares about them (empathy), they tend to trust them (see Fig. 1).

Each element individually is important and if one is missing, there is compromised overall trust. So how does a leader demonstrate these components?

Fig. 1 The Trust Triangle. (Adapted from 'Begin with Trust', Frei and Morriss [1])

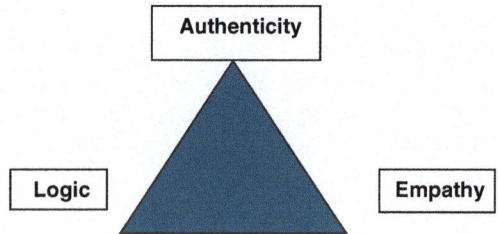

Authenticity

Authenticity is both the easiest and the hardest element. It needs to begin with self-awareness and self-reflection. Leaders become more authentic when they know who they are, what they value, what they are good at and how others see them. Intrinsically linked to authenticity is vulnerability. We all make mistakes—even leaders, and even very powerful, high-profile leaders. Leaders who can admit mistakes and even more importantly recognise the impact of those mistakes, will come across as honest, and ultimately trustworthy.

Logic

Logic and reliability are vital. People don't expect their leaders to know everything, but they do need confidence in their leader's ability to do their job. Leaders need to use the best evidence to support their ideas and be across industry best practices. Leaders need to ensure they 'walk the walk' as well as 'talk the talk'—people will quickly lose faith in a leader who can't do both.

Empathy

Empathy is really the icing on the trust cake. It could be argued that leaders need a certain amount of ego and confidence to achieve and hold the positions that they do, but getting the balance between ego and empathy is critical. Leaders need to have a genuine sense of responsibility and empathy for those that report to them and demonstrate that they care about those that work hard to make their leaders look good.

Other Gems

- Choose the relish, choose the noodles and choose the crumb-laden pastries—what's the worst that could happen?

References

1. Frei, F. X., & Morriss, A. (2020). Begin with trust. *Harvard Business Review*. https://hbr.org/2020/05/begin-with-trust
2. Zak, P. (2017). The neuroscience of trust. *Harvard Business Review*. https://hbr.org/2017/01/the-neuroscience-of-trust

It's Not All About You

Stephanie Jones

Leadership Pearl

Put your own ego aside and remember who you are leading and why.

Scenario

A multi-disciplinary team in a medical department is required to evaluate access and flow performance and develop an improvement strategy. The Director of the Unit has a clear idea of the strategies that they want to implement and spends the workshop time presenting their own vision, criticising suggestions from others, talking over contributors, and becoming defensive when challenged on their ideas. The team is discouraged that the Director has made decisions without considering or acknowledging their contributions and has taken credit for a strategy that they don't support. The Director then presents their strategy to the Executive, which not surprisingly, is not well received. The Director returns to the team to try and change the strategy. Having received leadership coaching in the interim, the Director seeks input from the team, identifies key members to lead specific pieces of work, and decisively manages conflicts to reach acceptable resolutions. The Director invites the project leads to present directly to the Executive and acknowledges the team effort via communication within the organisation. The team feels valued and takes accountability for the change process to deliver a sustainable improvement strategy.

S. Jones (✉)
Department of General Medicine, Monash Health, Melbourne, VIC, Australia

Discussion

Ego is commonly defined as the sense of one's own self-worth. A certain amount of ego is required for a leader as a healthy sense of self results in the confidence to make decisions, take risks, and achieve goals [1, 2]. The ambitious drive associated with ego can enable achieving impactful change, as long as the ego is balanced with emotional intelligence, humility, and empathy [3], and ambition for the organisation and/or team rather than for themselves.

An overinflated ego can influence leaders to make decisions that are self-serving and ultimately detrimental to the function of the team that they are leading. A leader with an unhealthy ego will strive to prove themselves right, fail to listen to contributions from others, claim credit where it is not due, and find it difficult to share success with the team, undermining teamwork and engagement [2, 3].

The key to balancing ego in leadership is awareness and self-reflection. Being aware of the positives and negatives of ego and understanding how they play out in yourself and your reactions, allows you to check negative behaviours before they damage your working relationships. Reflecting on interactions that have gone well or gone badly with a lens on how your ego influenced your reactions allows you to plan different strategies for the future.

Everyone will have different triggers for when their ego kicks in. It might be reacting defensively when challenged or questioned, stepping in to micromanage a project if it's not being done the way you think it should be, interrupting contributors in meetings to give your own point of view, or congratulating yourself on a job well done without acknowledging the rest of the team. If you can recognise these patterns in yourself, you can take a breath before reacting and take a more balanced approach.

Build your emotional intelligence by actively listening with humility and empathy, accepting that you are not always right, and you still have much to learn [3]. Empower your team by developing their strengths and giving them accountability for results, while being available to them for advice and support. Be authentic in your interactions, admit when you could be wrong or when you need support or advice from someone else, and be humble about success, celebrating it with your team. Ask questions to understand your team's motivations and capacity e.g., "Tell me what is most important to you in this project?" and "What do you need from me in order to be successful?". Embrace the strength of your positive ego; your resilience, determination to succeed and your decisiveness, and use that strength to build a team that succeeds with you [2, 3]. Remember who you are leading and why; it's not all about you.

Other Gems

- Develop as a leader through reflection and learning.
- Treat your team as you would want to be treated, with respect, sincerity and kindness.

- Don't be overly humble otherwise your team may lose confidence in you; it's all about balance.
- Find people who challenge you (and your ego).

References

1. Gundrabura, A. (2023, November). The good and bad of leadership ego. linkedin.com
2. Percy, S. (2023, May). A blessing and a curse: How can leaders manage their egos? forbes.com
3. McDonald, S. (2022, June). How to not let your ego get in the way of good leadership. *LeadershipHQ*.

Recruiting Excellent Staff

Kwang Lim

Leadership Pearl

Use your networks to recruit excellent staff. Spend more time on recruiting and less on performance management.

Scenario

You are interviewing two candidates for a consultant position. Both look good on paper and have excellent Curricula Vitae (CVs). The first candidate is very confident and answers all questions immaculately. The second candidate is very nervous and stumbles over some answers. She also pauses to think when asked about specific scenarios although her answers are reasonably thoughtful. The panel is unanimous and are very impressed by the first candidate. His references are good, and he is offered the position.

The consultant commences work and turns out to be a difficult doctor to work with. While no one doubts his clinical acumen, he is demanding and dismissive of other opinions. His junior doctors feel unsupported. In contacting his references again, the referees indicate that there may have been some relationship issues with other staff but felt that given his excellent research and clinical skills they did not want to provide a negative reference.

K. Lim (✉)
Royal Melbourne Hospital, Department of Medicine, University of Melbourne, Melbourne, VIC, Australia

© The Author(s), under exclusive license to Springer Nature Singapore Pte Ltd. 2025
R. Junckerstorff, S. Baqar (eds.), *Leadership Pearls in Healthcare*,
https://doi.org/10.1007/978-981-96-4233-5_15

Discussion

In his book *Hire for Attitude*, Mark Murphy explains that 46% of new hires don't stay in the job for longer than 18 months [1]. In almost all instances, the cause for new hire failures is attitude and emotional intelligence rather than technical skills. This means, choosing candidates based on their CVs which typically provides a summary of a candidate's qualifications, work experience, and skills may be problematic as the CV doesn't capture the full context of their achievements or the environment in which they worked.

Jim Collins, a well-known management consultant and author, has a clear philosophy on hiring. Collins emphasises the importance of getting "the right people on the bus" and getting them in the "right seats" (placing them in roles which suit their skillset and enables them to excel). Some key points of his hiring philosophy are as follows [2]:

First Who, Then What

Collins argues that the first priority of successful companies is not deciding what to do, but rather who will be doing it. The right people will figure out the right path.

Right People in the Right Seats

It's not enough to have the right people on the bus; they must also be in the right seats. This means ensuring that employees are in roles which fit their requisite strengths.

Character Over Credentials

Focus on intrinsic qualities such as values, work ethic, attitude, and willingness to learn, which are often better predictors of long-term success rather than specific skills or experiences.

Rigour in the Hiring Process

Be highly selective in the hiring process, even if it means taking more time to fill a position.

Don't settle for a less-than-ideal candidate simply to fill a position quickly.

Culture of Discipline

Hire people with self-discipline who do not need to be tightly managed.

Focus on Long-Term Fit and Growth Potential

Look for candidates who not only fit the current role but also have the potential to grow within the organisation.

Other Gems

- Go after the cream. As Steve Jobs said, a small team of A+ players can run circles around a giant team of B and C players.
- Use your networks to recruit. Often members of your team know other good clinicians. Staff generally tend to recommend people they would like to work with.
- Don't be afraid to use your networks to try and establish an applicant's values, integrity and their ability to work in a team. This is often hard to gauge during an interview and even from reference checks (as evidenced by the scenario presented).
- Don't hesitate to call people you think are good and suitable for a role even if they appear happily employed elsewhere. I have recruited successfully by contacting clinicians who have unexpectedly been considering other opportunities.

References

1. Murphy, M. (2011). *Hiring for attitude: A revolutionary approach to recruiting and selecting people with both tremendous skills and superb attitude.* McGraw-Hill.
2. Collins, J. (2001). *Good to great: Why some companies make the leap… and others don't.* Random House Business Books.

Part III

Interprofessional Relationships and Collaboration

Create Discussion by Not Saying "No"

Stephanie Jones

Leadership Pearl

Ask "how can I help?" before saying "no."

Scenario

The Director of a Medical Unit is overwhelmed, with numerous projects being developed to improve quality indicators, requiring multiple stakeholder meetings, finalisation of change impact processes, and writing of procedures. One of the senior staff in the Department approaches the Director saying that she thinks there is a better way to progress one of the innovations and wants to sit down and explain it in detail. The Director responds by saying, "No, we already have a plan for this." The senior staff member leaves, disgruntled, and complains to her colleagues that the Director doesn't listen or value the contribution of the senior team. When the innovations roll out, the senior team are not engaged and criticise the processes that have been developed. The Director is frustrated that all their hard work is not showing results and is sitting dejected in their office when the senior staff member approaches them again and starts to explain what they think has gone wrong with the roll out and how it could work better. The Director takes a deep breath and asks, "How can I help you to develop this idea?" What follows is a discussion from a perspective that the Director had not previously considered and identifies a number of the Director's preconceptions, as well as a lot of potential resources that the Director was not aware of. By way of this collaborative conversation, the Director is able to engage the senior staff member in taking a role in the development of the

S. Jones (✉)
Department of General Medicine, Monash Health, Melbourne, VIC, Australia

project, substantially reducing their own workload, and creating a sense of camaraderie between them and the senior team as they develop the rollout plan together.

Discussion

Leaders are often overwhelmed, with the responsibility of their role, the potentially serious repercussions of their decisions, and the constant influx of requests from their team, their managers and their clients. There is a large volume of wisdom that instructs or guides the leader on how to protect themselves from an unmanageable workload or unreasonable requests by learning to say "no."

There is an art to saying "no" and many of the tips are basic common decency; be nice about it, be positive, be empathetic to the person making the request, be honest about why you can't take on that request and be helpful by offering an alternative or directing the request to someone who has the capacity to help. A well-considered "no", takes into account your priorities, allows you to be available for the most important tasks, and allows you to focus. Saying "no" when you are at capacity protects you from burnout and allows you to reserve your energy and remain resilient [1].

However, it must be remembered that "no" is a negative word and it must be used carefully. A knee-jerk "no" to a request or suggestion does not allow further conversation or a deeper understanding of the situation and can create hostility [2].

Even more importantly, as a leader, your role is to empower your team to reach their goals. Developing the ability to deeply understand and justify a request focuses your team on the goal and to think critically about how to get there. Shutting people down by saying "no" takes away their drive and engagement, and ultimately makes your job more difficult as you rob yourself of the opportunity to use the skills, knowledge, and passion that your team brings to the job.

It may help to use a framework to assess your best response to a request:

- Understand the ask.
- A considered "no" if the request is impossible to agree to.
- An effective "yes" to add value [3].

In understanding the ask, it is necessary to ask specific questions to clarify what is being asked and why, what resources are required, what the timeline looks like, and what the outcomes will be. If the ask is simple, this can be accomplished in a brief conversation; make sure that you both agree on what is being asked and offered. If the ask is more complex, it is useful to stipulate what information you need to progress the request and document those expectations.

A considered "no" may be because the ask cannot be accommodated due to rules or procedures, ethical considerations, or a valid lack of capacity. In saying "no" it is important to share the justification with the person making the request so that they can understand why it is not possible and to help them to potentially reframe the request in a way that can be accommodated.

An effective "yes" also deserves an explanation to the requester, to clearly set the request into the framework of the goals and vision of the team, the prioritisation of the request, and to set some ground rules about how this ask will be achieved.

There are endless requests made of leaders; some big, such as setting up a new project, and some small, like accepting a patient referral. The time spent in responding to these requests should be commensurate with the size of the ask, however the principles are the same; engage in a meaningful conversation to understand each other, whether the answer is a considered "no" or an effective "yes".

Other Gems

- If the request cannot be accommodated right now, make sure your "no" gives the option to re-explore in the future.
- It's harder to recant a hasty "no" and rebuild trust, than it is to take the time to lay the foundations for an effective "yes".
- Asking "how can I help?" doesn't mean you have to take on the work; it can mean "how can I help set you up to be successful in your ask?"

References

1. Stall, S. (2023, September). The power (and art) of saying no. https://leadershipcircle.com/power-of-saying-no/
2. Myatt, M. (2011, December). One word that will transform you as a leader. Forbes.com.
3. Tulgan, B. (2020, September-October). Learn when to say no. *Harvard Business Review*.

Embracing Servant Leadership

Nick Coatsworth

Leadership Pearl

In healthcare, where teamwork and collaboration are essential, adopting a servant leadership approach can significantly enhance team dynamics and patient outcomes.

Situation 1

Throughout my career, I've found myself in leadership positions at a relatively young age compared to my peers. For instance, as the Director of a clinical department in a major hospital, all the other clinicians in the department I was leading were more senior and experienced. Adopting a servant leadership approach was crucial. This involved adopting the principle of leadership *for* them, not *over* them. It meant being accessible, approachable, and actively seeking advice from my more experienced colleagues.

Situation 2

When I led the second Australian Medical Assistance Team to the Philippines after Typhoon Haiyan, a leadership style, characterized by humility and service, helped build trust and cohesion among team members, all of whom were leaders in their own right. In medicine, our training conditions us to be independently minded practitioners capable of defending our clinical positions. This independent spirit can

N. Coatsworth (✉)
School of Regulation and Global Governance, Australian National University,
Canberra, ACT, Australia

R. Junckerstorff, S. Baqar (eds.), *Leadership Pearls in Healthcare*,
https://doi.org/10.1007/978-981-96-4233-5_17

make it challenging to lead other doctors if one does not adopt a servant leadership approach. To "herd the cats," as the saying goes, one must be willing to serve, support, and uplift one's colleagues. This involves understanding the unique strengths and challenges each team member faces and providing the necessary support to help them excel.

Discussion

Servant leadership is a concept that resonates deeply in the healthcare environment. It is particularly relevant when one is in a position where they are considered "first among equals." This type of leadership emphasises the leader's role as a servant to their team, focusing on the needs of others, and helping them to develop and perform to as a high a level as possible. Servant leadership requires humility, empathy, and a genuine commitment to the well-being of others. In practical terms, this might mean taking on tasks that are not typically associated with leadership, such as spending time on the frontline, seeking out, listening to and addressing the concerns of team members, and providing the necessary resources and support for their success. It also involves recognising and celebrating the achievements of your team, fostering a culture of appreciation and mutual respect.

In the context of the COVID-19 pandemic, my role as Deputy Chief Medical Officer required a servant leadership approach. Engaging with the Australian community through various media platforms and spearheading the national COVID-19 vaccination campaign involved clear communication and a focus on serving the public. This was not just about delivering information but about addressing fears, providing reassurance, and guiding the nation through a complex and unprecedented crisis. A useful tool was using reflection, where relevant, on how the challenges were affecting me personally.

Servant leadership is a well-suited style in healthcare because our work is inherently oriented to serving others. Whether we are caring for patients, supporting colleagues, or working with administrative staff, the principles of servant leadership can help create a more supportive and effective working environment. Importantly, by being seen to prioritise the needs of others, one will likely find that their team is more inclined to work toward achieving the leader's goals.

In addition to practical actions, servant leadership also involves fostering an environment of continuous learning and growth. This means encouraging team members to pursue professional development opportunities, providing constructive feedback, and creating a culture where learning from mistakes is valued. Where I have found success as a leader, it has always involved taking the time to create that environment. It is time-consuming and so needs to be consciously attended to during the working week.

Ultimately, servant leadership is about embodying the values of humility, empathy, and service in every aspect of our work. It is a reminder that effective leadership is not about being above others but about being with them, supporting them, and working alongside them to achieve common goals. Whether in a disaster zone, during a pandemic, or in everyday clinical practice, this principle has been a guiding force in my approach to leadership and has helped me build strong, resilient, and effective teams.

Other Gems

- Actively seek to understand the priorities of those you lead and incorporate them into your own goals as a leader.
- When leading other leaders, the most effective approach centres around humility and empathy.

Get to Know the People You Work With

Kwang Lim

Leadership Pearl

Building trust and knowing your staff personally helps you professionally.

Scenario

One of the junior doctors has been taking a lot of sick leave recently. She had previously been a very high-performing doctor. She completed her rotation, and her supervising consultant thought nothing more of it until she approached the consultant for a reference towards the end of the year. On further discussion it appeared that she had been experiencing severe symptoms during her rotation and ended up requiring emergency surgery. She then required time off work for an extended period. This came as a great shock to the consultant, as firstly they felt that they had not provided the support she required at the time, and secondly, they had thought of themselves as very approachable.

In response to this situation, the consultant now invites their team for a weekly coffee. This enables them to find out any issues the junior doctors may be experiencing as well as allowing conversations about their background, interests and in some cases career trajectories. By building these relationships, it enables the more junior members of the team to be more open with any issues they have been experiencing. It also means the consultant can render assistance as issues arise.

K. Lim (✉)
Royal Melbourne Hospital, Department of Medicine, University of Melbourne, Melbourne, VIC, Australia

Discussion

Trust is the foundation of a successful team. When leaders take the time to get to know their staff on a personal level, it fosters an environment of support, trust, and open communication. Staff who feel trusted and valued are more likely to share their ideas, concerns, and feedback. It also enables them to bring their true selves to work. According to the author Simon Sinek, trust is "built between meetings" through small, consistent interactions that accumulate over time [1]. The random conversations that occur, in themselves, are fairly innocuous, but together build a picture of the people you are interacting with and over time, builds a relationship of trust.

Neuroscience experiments show that when people intentionally build social ties at work, their performance improves. A nationally representative survey of working adults in the United States in 2016 showed that both organisational trust and having a sense of purpose at work increased productivity and earnings by employees, reduced job turnover, improved job satisfaction, and made people happier and healthier [2]. Similarly, a study performed by Google found that managers who "express interest in and concern for team members' success and personal well-being" outperform others in the quality and quantity of their work [3].

Other Gems

- Junior doctors do not like to be micromanaged, but do appreciate career advice.
- When staff trust their leaders, they are more open to feedback as they feel that the leader is on their side.
- Knowing your staff or juniors personally also allows you to be more invested in their success leading to greater job satisfaction.

References

1. Sinek, S. (2014). *Leaders Eat Last*. Portfolio Penguin.
2. Johannsen, R., & Zak, P. J. (2021, January). The neuroscience of organizational trust and business performance: Findings from United States working adults and an intervention at an online retailer. *Frontiers in Psychology, 11*(11), 579459. https://doi.org/10.3389/fpsyg.2020.579459. PMID: 33505331; PMCID: PMC7830360
3. Garvin, D. A. (2013, December). "How Google sold its engineers on management." R1312D. *Harvard Business Review, 91*(12), 74–82.

Expertise: Rehearse, Refine, Repeat

Christina Johnson

Leadership Pearl

Doing a good job is like learning to drive a car; it takes a lot of practice in a variety of conditions and a few near misses, saved by good supervision.

Scenario

Learning to drive a car takes a lot of time and practice. Young learner drivers are required to do 120 hours of practice before they take a driving test in Victoria, Australia. With my children, we started in an empty car park so my teenagers could learn the basics such as steering and gradual acceleration/deceleration with just a few hazards to avoid. Then we moved onto quiet roads, often early on a weekend morning, to become familiar with traffic lights, roundabouts, and the occasional other vehicle. As their proficiency increased, they advanced to driving at faster speeds, on busier roads, in various weather conditions, and with common distractions like having a conversation or the radio on. As the hours of practice mounted up, I gradually reduced the intensity of supervision and input. However I continued to watch carefully, as there were still occasions when they would misjudge a situation and I needed to intervene. For example, they might start pulling out in front of a vehicle that was coming faster than they realised or overestimate how long the amber traffic light would last as they approached a junction.

C. Johnson (✉)
Monash Doctors Education, Monash Health, Melbourne, VIC, Australia

School of Clinical Sciences, Faculty of Medicine, Nursing and Health Sciences, Monash University, Melbourne, VIC, Australia

© The Author(s), under exclusive license to Springer Nature Singapore Pte Ltd. 2025   81
R. Junckerstorff, S. Baqar (eds.), *Leadership Pearls in Healthcare*,
https://doi.org/10.1007/978-981-96-4233-5_19

Discussion

Virtually all of you will have had this experience of learning to drive. Even when your instructor clearly explained what to do, it was not easy to enact. It required multiple rehearsals, with the instructor offering tips, for you to create your own mental model on 'what needs to be done' and 'how to do it.' Everyone expects that learning to safely drive in a wide variety of situations takes hours of dedicated practice. At the start, it required full concentration as you attempted simple manoeuvres, which were performed clumsily. When you first attempted complex tasks, the instructor may have taken over some components to reduce the cognitive load. One example is merging onto a freeway. This high-risk manoeuvre combines acceleration up to high speed and avoiding multiple other cars as you change lanes. To begin with, I used to watch the upcoming traffic to identify a safe gap, while my learner driver focused on reaching the required speed and the path ahead. Once you are experienced, you can smoothly handle difficult traffic conditions and anticipate hazards. Yet even seasoned drivers struggle in a different context, such as driving overseas on the other side of the road.

I hope the 'learning to drive' narrative will help you to consider health professions training afresh. These principles apply to learning any new task or role. In clinical practice there are many tasks a doctor needs to learn while working on a hospital ward. As well as the core clinical care, they need to become proficient at summarising the ward round discussion in the medical notes, prioritising competing tasks across the day, explaining care to patients in a way they can understand, and responding to nurses' requests, to name just a few. Each of these tasks is complex with multiple factors that vary from one instance to the next. Yet it's common for consultants to get frustrated when a junior doctor cannot do a task perfectly, particularly if they have told the junior doctor how to do it once already. The learning curve for these cognitive skills is similar to procedural skills such as driving a car; it's just not as easy to see the factors considered or the outputs. You may have heard of the idea that it takes 10, 000 hours to become an expert. This arose from research by Ericsson in which he described the concept that expertise required many hours of deliberate practice [1, 2]. Try re-reading the first two paragraphs and applying it to a healthcare context.

"Tellin' Ain't Teaching"

A wonderful colleague of mine, Janita Keating, introduced me to the axiom "Tellin' ain't teaching". This highlights that if you give someone instructions, it does not mean they can now do it themselves. Our brains use mental schemas or 'blueprints' for concepts and tasks. These mental models link together all the relevant information so it can be swiftly retrieved as a single unit from our memories. Learning involves gradually refining these mental models. When we apply a concept or perform a task, we utilise the mental model to guide us. Components of the mental model that worked well are reinforced and any aspects that did not work well can be modified. Yet it requires attention and mental effort to problem-solve the issue. You need to work out exactly which bit is faulty and correct it. The processing system has a limited capacity so a person can only focus on revising one or two aspects at a time. So if a clinical performance evaluation covers too many points, the processing system can become overwhelmed, which thwarts learning. This refers to the concept of cognitive load [3]. Honing a mental model typically requires repeated cycles of rehearsal and revision, until the template works effectively (just like learning to smoothly and swiftly reverse into a car parking space).

Other Gems

- Just like teaching someone to drive a car, it's best to observe a person undertake a task and then discuss an improvement plan with them. The equivalent for mental tasks requires 'thinking out loud' i.e. asking them to describe their reasoning to make the process visible.
- Focus on how you can help the person to do it effectively themselves.
- Each time, focus on refining one or two aspects only.
- Teach 'the next step' along the learning curve and don't jump too far ahead to something too difficult.
- When you offer advice, make it a practical tip and explain the reasoning, so it's easier for the learner to apply it and understand the rationale.
- Ideally 'watch' the learner perform the task again to check they can enact the new version.

References

1. Ericsson, K. A. (2008). Deliberate practice and acquisition of expert performance: A general overview. *Academic Emergency Medicine, 15*. https://doi.org/10.1111/j.1553-2712.2008.00227.x
2. https://hbr.org/2007/07/the-making-of-an-expert
3. https://education.nsw.gov.au/content/dam/main-education/about-us/educational-data/cese/2017-cognitive-load-theory.pdf

Networking Without the Warm White Wine and Canapés

Sarah Lorentzen

Leadership Pearl

Make your network work for you—be clear about what you need a network for, when you need it and what you need it to achieve.

Scenario

We've all been there. The Royal Association of Thingumy Whatsit Annual Breakfast or networking drinks. Rubbery chipolatas, congealed scrambled eggs or for the evening option, warm cheap chardonnay and a goats cheese tart you could break a tooth on. Will I know anyone? What if I run into Adam Whatshisface… I may run the risk of being literally bored to DEATH. WHY. AM. I. HERE?

Discussion

The phrase 'networking' probably has a slightly negative connotation (see chipolata statement above), and indeed 'I hate networking' is a familiar refrain. However, with a quick Google search, lots of reputable people and organisations think it's a pretty good idea and vital to career growth [1]. And I kind of hate to say it, but they are probably right. However, there are a few things you can do to make it less of a painful process, help realise the potentially huge benefits and avoid the tooth-breaking goats cheese tarts.

S. Lorentzen (✉)
Monash Health, Melbourne, VIC, Australia

© The Author(s), under exclusive license to Springer Nature Singapore Pte Ltd. 2025   85
R. Junckerstorff, S. Baqar (eds.), *Leadership Pearls in Healthcare*,
https://doi.org/10.1007/978-981-96-4233-5_20

Define Your Purpose

Networking is not necessarily about getting your next job. Sometimes it might be about doing your current job better or finding a new source of information to help you in your current role. In fact, you might be already networking but not even know it! Before you start networking, it helps to define exactly what you want out of the experience. This will guide who you network with and the way in which you might go about networking. It's also helpful to note that networking doesn't just apply to our professional lives—it can also be helpful in our social and personal lives. So be clear as to what you need out of networking—maybe it *is* a new job, or maybe you just need some additional inspiration to do your current job, or maybe it's to find a new tennis club/work out which dog to buy/find the love of your life (yes speed dating is a form of networking).

The way in which you approach networking will depend on your purpose, however when your purpose is to find a new job, it may be helpful to be a little more 'intentional' about your networking. For example, you might dedicate some time each week to expand your network or at least identify the people you want to talk to or events you want to attend. It doesn't happen by osmosis or simply luck—you need to put in the effort to reap the reward.

Identify Your People

Once you're clear on your purpose, you can start formulating who's on your networking hit list. It's a good idea to do your research thoroughly at this point. Familiarise yourself with their online profile, website content, blogs, publications and recent events or activity. Only reach out if you have a relatively high degree of confidence that they might serve your purpose and if there is some chance that they might respond to you.

Another great way in identifying your people is to work your existing network for new contacts (i.e. 'hey Linda, do you know anyone who I could talk to about blah'). A personal connection will always bring a higher chance of a positive response than a cold call.

Look at Your Options

Thankfully these days, networking doesn't have to happen in a 3-star hotel—it can occur in a variety of ways, and plenty of them are online. You can find and research people using online professional platforms such as LinkedIn, read blogs and publications and attend online events. There are, however, still options for the social animals who prefer the face-to-face interactions (plus or minus the canapés). The advantage of these scenarios is that people can be somewhat obliged to talk to you, even if they are peering over your shoulder looking for someone they actually know.

A rejected professional advance or even simply being ignored is much more likely in the online world, but eventually you might get the 'yes' you've been after.

Putting it together, it's simply purpose, people, process.

Other Gems

- There are a raft of organisations that foster networking, especially for small business, such as the Victorian Small Business Network, Melbourne Business Network, Fresh Networking.
- For professional areas, networking opportunities can often be found along with seminars, workshops or presentations—you've already got a bunch of people with a common interest in a room. Don't rush off straight after the feature event—hang around and work the floor!
- If you have a specific purpose in mind, there will be an organisation out there that can help you. For example, I was looking for my first Board position and came across Women on Boards (www.womenonboards.net) who provide not only education and resources but also networking events specifically for women looking for Board roles.

Reference

1. Gino, F., Kouchaki, M., & Casciaro, T. (2016, May). Learn to love networking. *Harvard Business Review*.

Suspend Judgement to Improve Collaboration

Karen Livesay and Barbora de Courten

Leadership Pearl

Leaders demonstrate reflective insight into their own cultural beliefs and suspend judgement to approach differences with curiosity. From a perspective of curiosity and conscious reflection, leaders bypass inbuilt unconscious bias and instead find pathways to understanding and shared vision to enable collaboration.

Scenario

Jason, a paramedic, watched Alice an intern, complete intravenous cannulation on Mrs. Woods. Although the cannula was inserted on the first attempt, while removing the stylet, there had been blood leakage onto the trolley sheets and patient's skin and the cannula was not well immobilised. Jason approached Kelly, one of the Emergency Department (ED) registered nurses and nodding toward Alice said, "Why do they even let them work down here?"

Later in the day, the department was very busy and Jason arrived with a 47-year-old male who may have had a Transient Ischaemic Attack (TIA). There were no available beds in ED and Jason was unable to hand over the patient. He was agitated

K. Livesay
School of Health & Biomedical Sciences, STEM College, RMIT University, Melbourne, VIC, Australia

B. de Courten (✉)
School of Health & Biomedical Sciences, STEM College, RMIT University, Melbourne, VIC, Australia

Department of General Medicine, Monash Health, Melbourne, VIC, Australia

89

because he wanted his patient to have a Computed Tomography (CT) scan, and this could only happen under the care of the hospital. Kelly explained that if they could find a doctor to order and accompany the patient for the CT scan, it could be done before a bed became available. She then approached Alice, who eagerly agreed to help.

Jason and Alice took the patient to CT. Later, as Jason was leaving the emergency department, he stopped to thank Kelly. He admitted that he had little understanding of medical staff training and had unfairly judged Alice. He acknowledged his unconscious bias and expressed a desire to be more open-minded. Kelly smiled and explained that she had chosen Alice for the task because of her hard work and willingness to go above and beyond. She also pointed out that a single procedural skill does not define a medical intern's capabilities. They are doctors in training and all need to have the opportunity to learn basic procedural skills such as cannulation during their intern year.

Discussion

Suspension of Judgement

The concept of suspension of judgement has foundations in law with the presumption of innocence and in science where a hypothesis is tested and preconceived knowledge bracketed. However, in healthcare, the concept of unconscious or implicit bias and stereotypes is used to describe the problematisation of attitudes that can interfere with collaboration. Marcelin et al., assert that these implicit beliefs impact behaviours, interactions, and decision-making and can result in healthcare disparities [1]. This often foregrounds discussions of cultural safety and quality of care in underrepresented groups.

In the scenario presented, Jason didn't start from a perspective of belief. He formed a belief about an individual's worth in a particular context based on an observation. The observation showed an early phase of skill development that could have been accepted without a negative or positive connotation. Similarly, a patient with diabetes who admits to eating doughnuts for breakfast, demonstrates a behaviour but implies nothing about their own desire to improve their health outcomes. The suspension of judgement requires the individual to question whether their experience of another is inherently meaningful. Therapists practicing within the humanist tradition have upheld the relational requirement of unconditional positive regard first described by Rogers in the 1950s. In psychotherapy, the therapist approaches the client with warmth and affirmation regardless of what the client is sharing [2]. Suspension of judgement might be conceptualised as a midpoint on a continuum between unconditional positive regard and explicit bias and asks the provider to think about their reactions, pause their beliefs of meaning, and then 'check in' with the other person.

Curiosity

Curiosity is linked to a desire for exploratory behaviour that bodes well for learning, socialisation, job performance, decision-making and leadership amongst a longer list of attributes [3]. Reio and Wiswell describe curiosity related to socialisation, where employees learn things such as job requirements and cultural norms to adapt to their position and enhance success [4]. This cycle of curiosity is evident when a person joins a new organisation or is promoted to a new position but interestingly, curiosity is also seen in the continuing employees as they adapt to the newcomer. The motivation to be curious and learn occurs because of uncertainty [4]. It is the link to suspension of judgement, that enables curiosity. In a situation such as the scenario presented, Jason formed a belief about Alice that precluded his desire to think through and question his assumption about Alice. It was only the intervention of working together that unlocked a different belief and supported a new reflection. Feeling activated can support curiosity as we seek to manage uncertainty, but deliberate reflection can become a learned behaviour in which we deliberately suspend judgement.

Cross-cultural Knowledge

Curiosity as a precursor to learning has a strong association, however, curiosity has also emerged as an individual trait that supports developing cross-cultural competence [5]. While some people are naturally curious (personality trait) others can harness curiosity as a motivational state [5]. Cross-cultural knowledge is not static and an intersectional approach to understanding culture demonstrates the myriad of positions and diversities within a cultural group [6]. Understanding differences is more than learning schema and reviewing what is known about cultural groups. Mikhaylov reported that when students felt they had expert knowledge about a cultural group they showed less curiosity. Conversely, when they engaged in cultural knowledge sharing, their individual curiosity and motivation to learn about others increased [5]. Morell et al., described creating a critical incident to help students recognise their need to learn cultural competence [7]. In the scenario, Jason's critical reflection occurred when he needed to rely on Alice, unlocking his insight into not understanding medical training and the attributes of the medical intern.

Conclusion

In healthcare, differences exist across disciplines, education and hierarchies that are perpetuated by identity differences such as ethnicity, age, gender and sexuality. Where health professionals give in to unconsciously held beliefs, or use stereotypes as a proxy of understanding, communication and collaboration are impacted. Choosing to withhold one's beliefs in favour of deliberately thinking about what is unknown and assumed is a habit that fosters learning and understanding.

References

1. Marcelin, J. R., Siraj, D. S., Victor, R., Kotadia, S., & Maldonado, Y. A. (2019). The impact of unconscious bias in healthcare: How to recognize and mitigate it. *The Journal of Infectious Diseases, 220*(Supplement_2), S62–S73.
2. Suzuki, J. Y., Mandavia, A., & Farber, B. A. (2021). Clients' perceptions of positive regard across four therapeutic orientations. *Journal of Psychotherapy Integration, 31*(2), 129.
3. Wagstaff, M. F., Flores, G. L., Ahmed, R., & Villanueva, S. (2021). Measures of curiosity: A literature review. *Human Resource Development Quarterly, 32*(3), 363–389.
4. Reio, T. G., Jr., & Wiswell, A. (2000). Field investigation of the relationship among adult curiosity, workplace learning, and job performance. *Human Resource Development Quarterly, 11*(1), 5–30.
5. Mikhaylov, N. S. (2016). Curiosity and its role in cross-cultural knowledge creation. *International Journal of Emotional Education, 8*(1), 95–108.
6. Livesay, K., Lau, P., McNair, R., & Chiminello, C. (2017). The culturally and linguistically diverse SPs' evaluation of simulation experience. *Clinical Simulation in Nursing, 13*(5), 228–237.
7. Morell, V. W., Sharp, P. C., & Crandall, S. J. (2002). Creating student awareness to improve cultural competence: Creating the critical incident. *Medical Teacher, 24*(5), 532–534.

Team Harmony Brings Success

Karin Thursky and Ron Cheah

Leadership Pearl

Prioritise your team's harmony, and success will follow.

Scenario

You've landed your dream job as the Associate Director of Health Services Research at a major hospital and are responsible for establishing a new comprehensive organisation-wide health services research and implementation science

K. Thursky (✉)
Royal Melbourne Hospital Guidance Group, Melbourne, VIC, Australia

National Centre for Antimicrobial Stewardship, Department of Infectious Diseases, Melbourne Medical School, University of Melbourne, Melbourne, VIC, Australia

WHO Collaborating Centre for Antimicrobial Resistance, Doherty Institute, Melbourne, VIC, Australia

National Centre for Infections in Cancer, Peter MacCallum Cancer Centre, Melbourne, VIC, Australia

Centre for Health Services Research in Cancer, Peter MacCallum Cancer Centre, Melbourne, VIC, Australia

R. Cheah
Royal Melbourne Hospital Guidance Group, Melbourne, VIC, Australia

National Centre for Antimicrobial Stewardship, Department of Infectious Diseases, Melbourne Medical School, University of Melbourne, Melbourne, VIC, Australia

WHO Collaborating Centre for Antimicrobial Resistance, Doherty Institute, Melbourne, VIC, Australia

strategy. The goal is to ensure inter and multidisciplinary collaboration and build research workforce capacity.

Early in your tenure, you discover glaring organisational silos and a lack of interdisciplinary collaboration. Research projects are siloed by profession or department, resulting in duplication of work leading to an absence of a coordinated approach to health services research projects such as improved models of care. You observe that there's a strong medical hierarchy amongst the clinical researchers which has led to disharmony and inequality of access and participation across clinical groups including nurses, allied health, surgeons, and medical specialties.

Discussion

Team harmony must be prioritised as it is one of the most important factors for productiveness and collaboration. One strategy to ensure team harmony is to identify and avoid silos where possible, as this can not only contribute to wasteful duplication of effort, but more importantly, foster rivalry, discontentment, and a lack of understanding of broader organisational purpose.

The scenario above happens to be real, and this was my experience when I established a new department to integrate academics and clinician researchers. This process required significant effort in attracting key personnel and implementing a change management process to recruit staff from pre-existing teams. The situation was further complicated by the COVID-19 pandemic where many researchers were almost exclusively working from home.

I felt it was therefore imperative to thoroughly engage each staff member, one-on-one and face-to-face where possible, and build a vision where everyone was excited by the new opportunities and had a sense of purpose.

As leader, I was in a unique position to direct organisational wide strategy and had the capacity to implement my vision through the establishment of a new department where workplace harmony was the primary focus. It was essential to ensure access to new collaborative research opportunities and to be aware of and value each staff member's skills and career stage. Understanding the aspirations, potential and needs of each team member at a personal level ensured that each member of the team was able to work synergistically with like-minded colleagues, perform at their full potential and that their career goals aligned with or could be tailored to the organisation's objectives.

Our service has been described as 'world class' by external health service research reviewers due to the embedding of clinicians and health services researchers together and team members have overwhelmingly expressed their happiness to be part of this department. My experience has highlighted the powerful impact of team harmony on organisational success, proving that if the team is harmonious—happy, feel valued, and able to work collaboratively, they can achieve remarkable outcomes that benefit the entire organisation.

Other Gems

- Ignore existing barriers, be brave and persistent in your fight for equity of access.
- Do not underestimate the value of face-to-face meetings.
- Dedicate time to celebrate wins as a team.

Part IV

Systems Thinking and Strategic Planning

Know Your Limits and Extend Them

Stephanie Jones

Leadership Pearl

Recognise and articulate your own limitations and find someone to work with collaboratively who can address that skill gap. You'll get the job done and develop your own skills.

Scenario

The Director of a medical unit has been tasked with analysing key metrics for a presentation to the Board. The Director wants to present the unit and themselves in a positive light and takes control of the work to ensure it meets their exacting standards. As the date of the presentation looms, the Director is still faced with spreadsheets of data and no idea of how to present this in a meaningful way. The Director is used to leading as an expert in all aspects of the unit and feels embarrassed that they don't have the skills to complete this task; they are afraid of looking vulnerable or incompetent if they admit this to the team but also afraid of looking foolish or incompetent if they present poorly to the Board. They approach the administration assistant and ask them if they have the capacity to analyse the data, but he says that this is beyond his scope and recommends that the Director approach Business Intelligence (BI). The Director sets up a time with BI and over a couple of hours was not only able to have the data crafted into impactful graphics but also learns how to interpret and present the data. The Director realises that recognising and addressing their skill gap has led to a new collaborative relationship as well as an opportunity to expand their skills, and that no one thinks less of them as a leader.

S. Jones (✉)
Department of General Medicine, Monash Health, Melbourne, VIC, Australia

© The Author(s), under exclusive license to Springer Nature Singapore Pte Ltd. 2025   99
R. Junckerstorff, S. Baqar (eds.), *Leadership Pearls in Healthcare*,
https://doi.org/10.1007/978-981-96-4233-5_23

Discussion

While the scenario above relates to a very specific skill set, the principles of under-standing your strengths and weaknesses extend to all aspects of leadership. Leaders are not all knowing and omnipotent. An effective leader knows this and has the self-awareness and humility to recognise this. Self-awareness extends beyond knowing what you can and cannot do; it includes understanding yourself, your reactions, and triggers. Empathy, kindness, and patience are manifest in a leader who recognises their triggers. They are able to take a deep breath and respond mindfully, while a leader who portrays themselves as invulnerable may appear arrogant or unapproach-able. Developing self-awareness is deliberate; practice open-mindedness, focus, be self-disciplined, apologise when necessary, and actively seek feedback to enable reflection on yourself and your actions [1].

A good leader will be confident in their ability, and comfortable to admit when something is beyond their expertise. This honesty shows their team that they are authentic and human, and opens them to opportunities to expand their experience, both in skills and in the relationships that are developed when they reach out.

A self-aware leader engenders trust, teamwork and productivity through positive culture, effective delegation, and collaboration. A leader who tries to do it all, iso-lates themselves from the team, creates unrealistic expectations for themselves and will ultimately burn out.

People are unique, with different personalities and characteristics, and this indi-viduality extends to people who take on leadership roles. In broad terms, some people are "ideas people" who have a vision and can bring their team along on the journey, while others are "details people" who can harness reality to make ideas come to life [2]. Leaders are often "ideas people", although not exclusively, and they usually need "details people" to enact the ideas.

This being said, leaders should be encouraged to expand their skills outside their fundamental character type. It is not necessary for the leader to become proficient in the detail, but a basic understanding will help them to identify what is and is not within their scope, and to know who or what they need to complete the task. Through this, the leader can establish collaborative relationships with people within or out-side their team with expertise, delegate effectively, and ensure that delegated work is meeting the goals and visions of the team.

Finding someone who can complement your skills enhances everyone; you learn a few new tricks, the team trust your expertise and your ability to delegate, and the job gets done.

Other Gems

- Be confident and consistent in the things you know and curious about the things you don't.
- Get to know your team from the start; who they are and what they can do. Set yourself up to know the right person to ask to get something done.
- Leadership is growth—for you and your team.

References

1. Anziano, T. (2024, January). 10 tips for leaders to improve their self-awareness. businessnews-daily.com
2. Carter, H.R. (2002, July) Leaders must know their limitations. https://www.firehouse.com/home/article/10545308/leaders-must-know-their-limitations.

Knowing the Desired Outcome

Nick Coatsworth

Leadership Pearl

Preparation and strategic planning are key components of effective leadership.

Scenario

As Executive Director of Medical Services at Canberra Health Services, I often had to navigate complex discussions about clinician performance, behaviour, and practice. I had better results when I understood the administrative 'playing field' that I was operating in. That meant sufficient appreciation of human resource management policies, industrial relations and medical professional regulation, as well as knowledge of the individual or group I was working with and their desired aims and outcomes.

Discussion

A useful piece of advice is to never go into a meeting without knowing what you want the outcome to be. This principle applies to all types of meetings, whether it's a feedback meeting with a junior staff member, a hospital executive meeting, or a negotiation with a politician. Knowing the desired outcome ensures that you enter the meeting with clarity, focus, and a strategic approach, which is essential for achieving your goals.

N. Coatsworth (✉)
School of Regulation and Global Governance, Australian National University,
Canberra, ACT, Australia

R. Junckerstorff, S. Baqar (eds.), *Leadership Pearls in Healthcare*,
https://doi.org/10.1007/978-981-96-4233-5_24

Doctors, by nature of their training and practice, may not always be adept at these leadership skills and strategies. However, giving yourself time to prepare, understanding the desired outcome, and anticipating possible scenarios can provide a significant advantage. This involves war-gaming different scenarios, understanding the limits of your negotiating position, and being clear about your goals. By doing so, you can navigate complex discussions more effectively, manage conflicts, and achieve the desired outcomes.

Preparing for a meeting should not be a last-minute task. But whether its 15 minutes before or days in advance, the key is to ensure that it is done. This preparation helps you navigate complex discussions, manage conflicts, and achieve the desired outcomes more effectively. Thorough preparation also signals to others that you take the meeting seriously and are committed to achieving positive results. There are few things more confidence-sapping for a team member than meeting with you and seeing that you're underprepared.

Preparation can be a tedious and disruptive task, particularly when it involves learning new things on the fly. We often experience this as clinicians transitioning to become clinician leaders.

This can seem overwhelming at first and anyone who seeks to maintain a balanced portfolio of clinical and leadership work can't possibly achieve perfect knowledge of the legal and regulatory environment around them. In this common situation, finding others who can act either as mentors or advisors is essential. These can be individual relationships or as part of 'leadership groups' of clinical leaders.

In addition to sound preparation, it is important to be organised and be aware of future commitments that have the potential to be complex. For example, it is not good practice to allow yourself 30 minutes to fully understand the circumstances around a complicated performance management meeting. If something complicated is coming up, ensure adequate time is allowed to thoroughly prepare.

The principle of 'knowing the outcome' also applies to interactions beyond formal meetings. In everyday clinical practice, having a clear understanding of your goals and objectives helps in making better decisions and providing effective leadership. Whether it's a discussion with a colleague about a patient's care plan or a conversation with a junior staff member about their professional development, knowing the desired outcome ensures that the interaction is productive and aligned with your broader goals.

Other Gems

- Clarity on desired outcomes helps keep meetings and interactions focussed and on task.
- Preparation for meetings as a clinician leader is essential and may involve acquiring knowledge that you lack either through your own research or preferably via existing networks of people.

How to Write a Business Case: Data Rules

Kwang Lim

Leadership Pearl

Use data to craft your business case.

Scenario

A consultant physician had spent the last 3 years in the United Kingdom working in an innovative pre-operative service. This clinic produced outstanding results; patients who were admitted to hospital had shorter stays, had less complications and better outcomes. The consultant was very keen to set up a similar model of care in their new hospital in Australia. Despite compelling evidence demonstrating the success of this service, as the clinic was staffed by different specialities and allied health practitioners, she needed to obtain funding and the support of the relevant managers before she could progress her vision any further.

Consultants regularly tell their managers that their service will enhance the quality of care and provide better outcomes for patients. While this is what we as health care practitioners aspire to in all the care that we provide, the capacity to quantify this in terms of outcomes and the financial implications of it, often determine if a new service is supported by hospital executives. Doctors frequently say that they are not concerned about funding, but in the end, there is only one pot of money, and it is distributed in a way that aims to improve not just outcomes but efficiency.

K. Lim (✉)
Royal Melbourne Hospital, Department of Medicine, University of Melbourne,
Melbourne, VIC, Australia

Discussion

Writing a business case is critical in getting funding to develop a new service [1, 2].

1. Step one involves setting the scene; what is the status quo and what are the issues with the current service? Baseline data is helpful to illustrate the current situation.
2. Step two involves identifying the problem that you are trying to solve. Why should it be done now and what would happen if we retained the status quo? Using graphs and data is helpful to illustrate your point.
3. As part of the proposal, you need to describe the outcomes (both financial and patient-centred) you hope to achieve. The easiest way to present this data is to show evidence that you can improve revenue and access to services. For example, reducing inpatient complications will likely result in a shorter hospital length of stay, thereby freeing up beds. There is however a sweet spot with all diagnoses whereby an optimal length of stay gives you the maximum revenue per day. In Australia, there is a range of hospital length of stay (LOS) whereby you receive maximum income. For example, funding for an episode of care of uncomplicated pneumonia may be the same for patients admitted for 3 days as it is for those admitted for 7 days, making a LOS of 3 days the most profitable. A business case may also include outpatient services where revenue is derived from each patient contact.

In the above pre-operative clinic example, key targets included the reduction of length of stay, reduction in the surgical waiting list, and improved outcomes. The service also helped identify a cohort of patients undergoing elective surgery unnecessarily. Revenue was maximised through optimising outpatient templates and adding multidisciplinary loadings to each occasion of service.

The investment required is the cost of staff and equipment, projected over a 12-month period and the revenue you could potentially get (outpatient income) or the costs you could potentially save (bed days). Quality of care measures and strategic fit with the organisation are also important things to consider.

If you are required to present a business case, it may be useful to present a patient story. This helps contextualise the situation for non-clinical staff such as hospital executives. It emphasises the reality that we are aiming to improve the outcome and experience of real people, not just numbers on a page. In the end however, the numbers often decide the success of a proposal.

Most business cases are evaluated over a 12-month period to determine if funding should continue. One word of warning, it is best to be conservative: under promise and over deliver. I have been on the other end of over promising and under delivering and this is a sure-fire way to lose your funding and credibility!

Sometimes you can present more than one option. Present the pros and cons associated with each option, however, do make sure you have a preferred option. Remember that finance will evaluate the proposal based on the numbers provided.

Other Gems

- Build relationships with your executive, these relationships are critical both in terms of progressing your service and supporting you when things don't go as planned.
- Under promise and over deliver. This will help with continued funding and credibility with future proposals.

References

1. https://www.bhf.org.uk/informationsupport/publications/healthcare-and-innovations/business-case-toolkit%2D%2D-template
2. http://www.rcplondon.ac.uk/file/24771C:\Users\limk\AppData\Local\Microsoft\Windows\INetCache\Content.Outlook\UAB5S0NA\

Strike While the Iron Is Hot

Kwang Lim

Leadership Pearl

Prepare to adjust your strategies to grasp emerging opportunities.

"Humiliating to human pride as it may be, we must recognise that the advance and even the preservation of civilization are dependent upon a maximum of opportunity for accidents to happen." August von Hayek, winner of the 1974 Nobel Prize in Economics.

Scenario

In a community hospital, the leadership team are looking at growing the health service, particularly focusing on expanding subspecialty medicine. Currently, over 90% of medical admissions are admitted under General Medicine. There are three services that they are aiming to establish: an interventional Cardiology service, a Renal (kidney) service and an Oncology (cancer) service. Health services are funded based on activity and sometimes specific grants which can be historical in nature. As a relatively new hospital, they did not have the benefit of the established grants provided to some of the larger hospitals, so starting a new service involved a significant financial risk. Coincidentally, a federal election was to be held later in the year.

In the lead up to the election, a local community member had been very vocal about her daughter needing to travel long distances to receive chemotherapy for her cancer. As it turned out, she was a member and active fundraiser for the political

K. Lim (✉)
Royal Melbourne Hospital, Department of Medicine, University of Melbourne, Melbourne, VIC, Australia

party currently in power. Subsequently, an announcement was made by the incumbent Prime Minister promising one million dollars towards the establishment of a new cancer service.

That was all that was needed to set the wheels in motion. Plans were made that included the redevelopment of an existing ward, employing a head of oncology, other oncologists, a nursing team and developing protocols. This brought forward the growth of their health service by many years.

Discussion

When building a service, opportunities often arise when we are least expecting it. While planning is an important component of service building, the progress is not always linear. Be prepared to embrace opportunities even in areas where the preparation may not be advanced. Be aware that when funding is announced it is important to act on this opportunity. If an offer of financial support is not taken up, this may either delay the implementation of your service or your vision may in fact never come to fruition. The workforce and administration need to be flexible and adapt to changing circumstances.

As an example of being agile and adapting to changing circumstances, Professor Christian Busch tells a story of the potato washing machine. In China, a washing machine manufacturer started getting a lot of complaints from farming villagers about their washing machines. On further inquiry, they found that the farmers were trying to wash their potatoes in their washing machines and the filters were getting clogged up with dirt. Instead of counselling the farmers on their misuse of the washing machine, the manufacturer placed dirt filters in the machines and now potato washers have become one of their core products [1].

Busch describes serendipitous discoveries as smart luck. He discusses the science of serendipity as developing skills required to be open to opportunities [2]. In medicine, there are multiple examples of serendipitous discoveries; from medications such as penicillin and sildenafil (Viagra®), the latter being initially trialled for the treatment of chest pain, to the use of mRNA technology for the production of SARS-CoV-2 vaccines.

Other Gems

- Progress is rarely linear.
- Cultivating serendipity can be developed by building relationships within your service and between services, both in your hospital and in other hospitals both locally and internationally.
- Train your staff to be adaptable by constantly changing work practices and concepts, always looking for improvement.

References

1. Busch, C. (2020). *The Serendipity Mindset: The Art and Science of Creating Good Luck.* Penguin Random House; Wiseman (2003). *The Luck Factor.* Arrow.
2. Busch, C. (2024). Towards a theory of serendipity: A systematic review and conceptualization. *Journal of Management Studies., 61*(3), 1110–1151.

Taking a Step Back

Chris Gartside

Leadership Pearl

Find time to take a step back and get up on the "balcony"—, to have a systems / strategic view of what you are trying to achieve.

Scenario

A clinical manager is constantly involved in the day-to-day operations of their team. They are so immersed in the details that they struggle to see the bigger picture and long-term goals for the clinical area/division. After a particularly chaotic week, the manager decides to take a day away from their immediate tasks to reflect on the project's overall progress and future direction. By stepping back, they identify several areas for improvement and strategic opportunities that were previously overlooked due to their focus on daily tasks.

Discussion

Balancing day-to-day responsibilities with strategic oversight is crucial for effective leadership. Leaders often find themselves on the "dance floor," caught up in the immediate demands and operational details. However, it is equally important to take time to step onto the "balcony" to gain a broader perspective. This shift allows leaders to evaluate the system as a whole, ensuring that their efforts align with long-term goals and organisational vision [1, 2].

C. Gartside (✉)
Emergency Services and Access Division, Northern Health, Melbourne, VIC, Australia

Being constantly engaged in the minutiae can make it difficult to maintain a strategic focus. Leaders need to develop the ability to shift between different perspectives seamlessly. This concept is essential in various fields, whether in operations, clinical, education, or any other domain where leadership plays a pivotal role.

Operationally, leaders who fail to take a step back may find themselves reacting to immediate issues without considering their long-term impact. This reactive approach can lead to missed opportunities, inefficiencies, and a lack of direction. In contrast, leaders who regularly take time to reflect and strategise, are often better equipped to guide their organisation toward sustained success. They can anticipate trends, innovate, and position their organisations to capitalise on future opportunities [3].

Taking a strategic view involves several key elements.

First, it requires setting aside dedicated time for reflection and analysis. This means prioritising time to allow a leader to regularly step back from daily tasks. During these periods, leaders should focus on reviewing progress, evaluating current strategies, and identifying areas for improvement [4].

Additionally, effective strategic oversight requires gathering and analysing data. Leaders need access to accurate and timely information to make informed decisions. This might involve reviewing performance metrics, conducting market research, or seeking input from team members and stakeholders. By grounding their reflections in data, leaders can ensure that their strategic decisions are based on evidence rather than intuition alone [5].

Cultivating a strategic mindset also involves developing certain personal qualities. Curiosity, open-mindedness, and a willingness to challenge assumptions are essential traits for strategic leaders. These qualities enable leaders to explore new possibilities, question the status quo, and embrace change [6].

Moreover, strategic leaders are more likely to foster a culture of continuous improvement. By emphasising the importance of reflection and analysis, they encourage their teams to seek out opportunities for growth and innovation. This can lead to higher levels of engagement, creativity, and performance across the organisation [7].

However, achieving this balance is not without its challenges. One common obstacle is the pressure to prioritise immediate tasks over long-term planning. In fast-paced environments, leaders may feel that they cannot afford to take time away from day-to-day operations. Overcoming this challenge requires a conscious effort to prioritise strategic activities and recognise their importance for long-term success [8].

Other Gems

- *Schedule regular reflection periods to review progress and adjust strategies.* Regularly stepping back to reflect on progress and making necessary adjustments is a hallmark of effective leadership. Scheduling time for this reflection helps ensure that it becomes a consistent part of leadership practice, rather than an occasional activity.

- *Encourage and empower team members to take initiative and handle operational details, freeing you up to focus on strategic planning.* By empowering and upskilling team members to take ownership of operational tasks, leaders can create space for themselves to focus on higher-level strategic planning. This not only enhances team members' skills and engagement but also enables leaders to maintain a clear strategic vision.

References

1. Heifetz, R. A., & Laurie, D. L. (1997). The work of leadership. *Harvard Business Review, 75*(1), 124–134.
2. Goleman, D. (1998). What makes a leader? Harvard Business Review. Available: http://fs.ncaa. org/Docs/DIII/What%20Makes%20a%20Leader.pdf
3. Porter, M. E. (1996). What is strategy? Harvard Business Review. Available: https://iqfystage. blob.core.windows.net/files/CUE8taE5QUKZf8ujfYlS_Reading+1.4.pdf
4. Kaplan, R. S., & Norton, D. P. (1996). *The balanced scorecard: Translating strategy into action.* Harvard Business Review Press. Available: https://maaw.info/ArticleSummaries/ ArtSumKaplanNorton1996Book.htm
5. Davenport, T. H., & Harris, J. G. (2007). *Competing on analytics: The new science of winning.* Harvard Business Review Press. Available: https://www.researchgate.net/ publication/7327312_Competing_on_Analytics
6. Christensen, C. M., & Raynor, M. E. (2003). *The innovator's solution: Creating and sustaining successful growth.* Harvard Business Review Press. Available: https://www.academia. edu/25028182/Innovators_solution_revised_and_expanded_creating_and_sustaining_successful_growth
7. Edmondson, A. C. (2012). *Teaming: how organizations learn, innovate, and compete in the knowledge economy.* Jossey-Bass. Available: https://media.wiley.com/product_data/ excerpt/3X/07879709/078797093X-196.pdf
8. Covey, S. R. (1989). *The 7 habits of highly effective people: Powerful lessons in personal change.* Simon & Schuster. Available: https://ati.dae.gov.in/ati12052021_1.pdf

Part V
Innovation

Think Like a Visionary

Karin Thursky and Ron Cheah

Leadership Pearl

Think big from the start.

Scenario

Neutropenic fever is a common complication of cancer chemotherapy occurring in an estimated 5–30% of patients with solid tumours or lymphomas and in over 80% of patients with haematological malignancies or allogeneic haematopoietic stem

K. Thursky (✉)
National Centre for Antimicrobial Stewardship, Department of Infectious Diseases, Melbourne Medical School, University of Melbourne, Melbourne, VIC, Australia

RMH Guidance Group, Royal Melbourne Hospital, Melbourne, VIC, Australia

WHO Collaborating Centre for Antimicrobial Resistance, Doherty Institute, Melbourne, VIC, Australia

Centre for Health Services Research in Cancer, Peter MacCallum Cancer Centre, Melbourne, Australia

National Centre for Infections in Cancer, Peter MacCallum Cancer Centre, Melbourne, Australia

R. Cheah
National Centre for Antimicrobial Stewardship, Department of Infectious Diseases, Melbourne Medical School, University of Melbourne, Melbourne, VIC, Australia

RMH Guidance Group, Royal Melbourne Hospital, Melbourne, VIC, Australia

WHO Collaborating Centre for Antimicrobial Resistance, Doherty Institute, Melbourne, VIC, Australia

© The Author(s), under exclusive license to Springer Nature Singapore Pte Ltd. 2025
R. Junckerstorff, S. Baqar (eds.), *Leadership Pearls in Healthcare*,
https://doi.org/10.1007/978-981-96-4233-5_28

cell transplant recipients. It is associated with significant morbidity and mortality [1, 2].

Recognising the importance of this common yet potentially life-threatening clinical syndrome, I applied for and successfully received a relatively small service improvement grant to develop an ambulatory program for the management of neutropenic fever across five cancer hospitals. In the initial stages of program, I identified very little consistency in existing practices, and multiple touch points whereby cancer patients were being managed, including emergency departments, outpatient departments, hospital wards and chemotherapy day units. More concerningly, there was poor recognition of sepsis as a major complication of neutropenic fever.

At this point, I realised that I was at a crossroad. I could work with what I had been given and deliver a program for local improvement, or pivot and scale up to develop a comprehensive solution for a more widespread impact.

Discussion

It is essential to consider the potential impact of your research or initiatives, and what would happen if there was widescale adoption. This is about imagining the future, considering the implementability of your idea, and thinking big.

In this scenario, I chose the latter of the two options at the proverbial fork in the road. This is because I knew if my initiative could be applicable to all patients, not just to patients at my hospital, it could positively impact many more lives. I approached the funder to request funding to develop a guideline for *all* Australian hospitals instead of just focusing on one group of hospitals. The funders were supportive of this, and we proceeded to engage key stakeholders nationally to develop our country's first consensus guidelines: The Australian consensus guidelines for the management of neutropenic fever in adult cancer patients [3]. This remains the Australian standard of care.

Concurrently, I convened a sepsis working group within my hospital to develop a pathway to improve sepsis recognition. My priority was to ensure that the outcome from this work could be adopted widely, and to achieve this, I ensured that stakeholders were sufficiently represented as part of this committee. The committee was comprised of senior nurses, ICU and infectious diseases clinicians and hospital executives. All members were required to consider barriers and facilitators for effective sepsis recognition and management across all hospital areas from their unique perspectives. The local impact from our work was significant. We observed a 50% reduction in mortality and ICU admission, reduced length of stay, and demonstrated cost-effectiveness [4]. Most importantly, our findings confirmed that this pathway was equally effective in neutropenic and non-neutropenic patients, making it suitable for any hospital setting [4]. A key factor of our success was that the pathway was nurse initiated, and that for the first time, nurses felt empowered to advocate for early sepsis management of their patient. As result of our big picture approach, our program was later adopted and funded for implementation at another major hospital, and eventually further funded and scaled to 23 hospitals statewide as the "Think Sepsis Act Fast Program" [5].

Other Gems

- A larger impact can be made with a similar amount of effort when you adopt a big-picture perspective from the beginning.
- Empower a true multidisciplinary approach, encouraging program leads from other disciplines beyond the medical workforce.
- Consider the practicality and implementability of any solution to ensure scalability.

References

1. Zimmer, A. J., & Freifeld, A. G. (2019). Optimal management of neutropenic fever in patients with cancer. *Journal of Oncology Practice, 15*(1), 19–24.
2. Douglas, A., Thursky, K., & Slavin, M. (2022). New approaches to management of fever and neutropenia in high-risk patients. *Current Opinion in Infectious Diseases, 35*, 500–516.
3. Lingaratnam, S., Slavin, M. A., Koczwara, B., Seymour, J. F., Szer, J., Underhill, C., & Thursky, K. A. (2011). Introduction to the Australian consensus guidelines for the management of neutropenic fever in adult cancer patients, 2010/2011. *Internal Medicine Journal, 41*(1b), 75–81.
4. Thursky, K., Lingaratnam, S., Jayarajan, J., Haeusler, G. M., Teh, B., Tew, M., Venn, G., Hiong, A., Brown, C., Leung, V., & Worth, L. J. (2018). Implementation of a whole of hospital sepsis clinical pathway in a cancer hospital: Impact on sepsis management, outcomes and costs. *BMJ Open Quality, 7*(3).
5. Safer Care Victoria. (n.d.). *Think Sepsis.* Act fast. Available from: https://www.safercare.vic.gov.au/best-practice-improvement/improvement-projects/medications-treatment-infection-prevention/think-sepsis-act-fast

Revolutionising Healthcare: Partnering with Users for Better Solutions

Barbora de Courten, Mary Lam, and Karen Livesay

Leadership Pearl

Leaders work empathically with end-users to co-design health solutions using human-centred design approaches.

Scenario

Dr. Price, a senior geriatrician, was tasked with leading the development of a medical appointment reminder system (mobile app) for a chronic disease outpatient clinic in a tertiary hospital, with a particular focus on elderly patients. The primary objective was to enhance patient attendance at scheduled appointments and reduce the incidence of failure to attend (FTA) in the clinic which was currently more than 30%.

Initially, Dr. Price collaborated closely with the hospital's Information Technology (IT) department to design and implement the new system. Despite the ambitious six-month timeframe, the system was successfully developed and launched. However, post-launch, the adoption rate among elderly patients was only

B. de Courten (✉)
School of Health & Biomedical Sciences, STEM College, RMIT University, Melbourne, VIC, Australia

Department of General Medicine, Monash Health, Melbourne, VIC, Australia

M. Lam · K. Livesay
School of Health & Biomedical Sciences, STEM College, RMIT University, Melbourne, VIC, Australia

© The Author(s), under exclusive license to Springer Nature Singapore Pte Ltd. 2025   123
R. Junckerstorff, S. Baqar (eds.), *Leadership Pearls in Healthcare*,
https://doi.org/10.1007/978-981-96-4233-5_29

20%, lower than expected. A significant number of elderly patients continued to miss their appointments, with only a small proportion utilising the system.

Recognising the financial and operational implications of missed appointments, the hospital administration decided to engage external consultants to address this issue. They invited a design specialist and embarked on a user-centric journey.

Understanding the importance of involving end-users in the design process, consultants trained in human-centred design methods worked with Dr. Price and patients, their families, and other healthcare and administrative staff to develop empathy maps using personas. An empathy map is a tool that provides a series of prompts to identify a target consumer's thoughts, feelings, motivations, desires, and needs and often can redefine a problem through a consumer lens. This approach provided a comprehensive understanding of patient needs, and the challenges associated with managing appointments. Armed with these insights, Dr. Price formulated a precise problem statement that accurately represented the patients' needs.

Expanding the collaboration beyond the IT department, Dr. Price actively involved relevant stakeholders—administrators, nurses & allied health providers, patients, and their families—in the ideation, prototyping, and testing stages. Their diverse perspectives enriched the solution.

In contrast to the initial rushed development, Dr. Price adopted an iterative approach. The extended timeline allowed for thorough testing, feedback integration, and ongoing enhancement. The team refined the system until it met the unique needs of elderly patients.

The results were significantly positive. Both patients and hospital staff welcomed the improved appointment reminder system. The frequency of missed appointments notably decreased to less than 5%, leading to improved patient outcomes.

Discussion

In health innovation, co-designing solutions with end-users has become a fundamental approach. At the heart of this collaborative process lies an empathic understanding of users' needs.

Understanding User Needs

The process of co-design is rooted in empathy. By incorporating end-users, we can achieve a more profound understanding of their needs, preferences, and barriers [1]. Human centred design ensures that the developed solutions are genuinely centred on the user.

Precise Problem Statement Development

Human-centred design helps to redefine a problem and enables a leader to better understand the end-users of a potential health solution or innovation [2]. Involving all users and stakeholders ensures that the problem statement mirrors the real-world scenario and aligns with the needs of the different users of the future solution.

Ideation and Stakeholders Engagement

Human-centred design goes beyond the confines of the development team. By including all relevant stakeholders, the team in the above scenario used human-centred design and was able to explore innovative solutions by considering a range of viewpoints and novel ideas [3].

Iterative Prototyping and Testing

In contrast to the initial hurried development, human-centred design embraces an iterative approach. Iteration ensures that the solution evolves based on real-world usage and user feedback.

Conclusion

Human-centred design encourages collaboration, empathy, and iterative refinement. It transforms technological solutions from mere tools into valuable assets that genuinely meet user needs. Dr. Price's experience highlights the crucial role of empathic human centred design in the development of healthcare technology (Table 1).

Table 1 The Key Components of Human-Centred Design

Understanding user needs	The development of personas and empathy maps enabled Dr. Price to better understand the patients' and staff's challenges, emotions, and experiences associated with managing appointments.
Precise problem statement development	Human-centred design allowed Dr. Price to formulate a new problem statement that echoed the patients' concerns about ease of use and also considered insights from healthcare workers and administrative staff interacting with the system.
Ideation and stakeholder engagement	Dr. Price actively involved administrators, nurses, allied health practitioners and patients and their families in the process. Their varied perspectives enriched the ideation process.
Iterative prototyping and testing	Dr. Price's readiness to invest time beyond the initial 6 months allowed for comprehensive testing and the integration of feedback.

References

1. Pallesen, K. S., Rogers, L., Anjara, S., De Brún, A., & McAuliffe, E. (2020). A qualitative evaluation of participants' experiences of using co-design to develop a collective leadership educational intervention for healthcare teams. *Health Expectations, 23*(2), 358–367. https://doi.org/10.1111/hex.13002
2. Bird, M., McGillion, M., Chambers, E. M., Dix, J., Fajardo, C. J., Gilmour, M., Levesque, K., Lim, A., Mierdel, S., Ouellette, C., Polanski, A. N., Reaume, S. V., Whitmore, C., & Carter, N. (2021). A generative co-design framework for healthcare innovation: Development and application of an end-user engagement framework. *Research Involvement and Engagement, 7*(1), 12. https://doi.org/10.1186/s40900-021-00252-7
3. Sanz, M. F., Acha, B. V., & García, M. F. (2021). Co-design for people-centred care digital solutions: A literature review. *International Journal of Integrated Care, 21*(2), 16. https://doi.org/10.5334/ijic.5573

Be Inquisitive

Chris Gartside

Leadership Pearl

While you do not always need to provide the solution, it is important that you always ask the questions others might be too afraid to ask. This in turn helps form ideas and helps teams to better understand the challenges before determining the solution.

Scenario

As a member of the hospital's quality improvement committee, you are involved in meetings at which a high rate of hospital-acquired infections (HAIs) is on the agenda to be discussed. During these meetings, the committee members are reluctant to speak up, fearing their questions or suggestions might be dismissed. The chairperson of the committee continues to move through the agenda without addressing the high rate of infections. One member of the committee recognises the other members' hesitations and suggests a more inclusive and inquisitive approach. It is then suggested and endorsed that each meeting will open by asking questions like, "Does anyone have any safety first items they wish to elevate and discuss?" As a result, the committee uncovers several previously overlooked issues, that would not have previously been elevated during the meeting or discussed due to a reluctance to speak up. This approach has ensured that those who may not feel there is an opportunity to ask questions, had a space to do so.

C. Gartside (✉)
Emergency Services and Access Division, Northern Health, Melbourne, VIC, Australia

© The Author(s), under exclusive license to Springer Nature Singapore Pte Ltd. 2025   127
R. Junckerstorff, S. Baqar (eds.), *Leadership Pearls in Healthcare*,
https://doi.org/10.1007/978-981-96-4233-5_30

Discussion

Inquisitiveness is a fundamental quality of effective leadership. By asking thoughtful and sometimes challenging questions, leaders can uncover underlying issues, stimulate innovative thinking, and drive continuous improvement. While providing solutions is a critical aspect of leadership, fostering an environment where questions are encouraged can be equally impactful [1, 2].

Asking questions serves several important functions in leadership. First, it helps to clarify understanding and ensure that everyone is on the same page. When leaders ask questions, they signal that it is acceptable and even desirable to seek clarification and probe deeper into issues. This can prevent misunderstandings and align the team's efforts toward common goals [3].

Secondly, questioning can help to identify problems that may not be immediately apparent. In many cases, team members may be aware of issues but may be reluctant to bring them up due to fear of criticism or a desire to avoid conflict. By asking open-ended questions, leaders can create a safe space for team members to voice their concerns and share their perspectives [4].

Additionally, asking questions can help to uncover the root causes of problems. Rather than addressing symptoms, leaders who ask the right questions can guide their teams to investigate and understand the underlying factors contributing to challenges. This deeper understanding is essential for developing sustainable solutions that address the core issues [5].

In addition to asking the right questions, an important skill of a leader is to practice active listening. When leaders ask questions, they must be prepared to listen attentively to the responses. This means giving team members the time and space to express their thoughts fully, without interrupting or steering the conversation. Active listening demonstrates respect and shows that the leader values their input [6].

It should be noted that leaders need to be mindful of their tone and body language when asking questions. An inquisitive approach should be supportive and non-threatening. A leader should avoid asking questions in a way that could be perceived as accusatory or critical. Instead, they should adopt a curious and open-minded position. This signals that they are genuinely interested in understanding different perspectives [7]. An inquisitive leadership style can also be particularly valuable during times of change or uncertainty. When teams are faced with complex challenges or navigating transitions, asking the right questions can help to clarify priorities, uncover new opportunities, and build a shared understanding of the path forward. Inquisitive leaders can guide their teams through uncertainty by fostering a sense of curiosity and encouraging a proactive approach to problem-solving [8].

Other Gems

- *Ask open-ended questions to encourage exploration and discussion.* Open-ended questions invite team members to share their thoughts and ideas in depth, leading to richer and more productive conversations.

- *Practice active listening and create a safe space for dialogue.* Active listening shows that the leader values team members' input and fosters an environment where everyone feels comfortable sharing their perspectives.
- *Use questioning to facilitate group discussions and brainstorming sessions.* Thought-provoking questions can stimulate dialogue and encourage collaborative problem-solving, leading to more innovative solutions.

References

1. Heifetz, R. A., & Laurie, D. L. (1997). The work of leadership. *Harvard Business Review, 75*(1), 124–134.
2. Goleman, D. (1998). What makes a leader? Harvard Business Review. Available: http://fs.ncaa.org/Docs/DIII/What%20Makes%20a%20Leader.pdf
3. Kouzes, J. M., & Posner, B. Z. (2017). *The leadership challenge: How to make extraordinary things happen in organizations* (6th ed.). Wiley. Available: https://nibmehub.com/opac-service/pdf/read/The%20Leadership%20Challenge_%20How%20to%20Make%20Extraordinary%20Things%20Happen%20in%20Organizations.pdf
4. Gardner, W. L., Avolio, B. J., Luthans, F., May, D. R., & Walumbwa, F. (2005). "Can you see the real me?" A self-based model of authentic leader and follower development. *Leadership Quarterly, 16*(3), 343–372.
5. Yukl, G. (2013). *Leadership in organizations* (8th ed.). Pearson. Available: https://nibmehub.com/opac-service/pdf/read/Leadership%20in%20Organizations%20by%20Gary%20Yukl.pdf
6. Edmondson, A. C. (2012). *Teaming: How organizations learn, innovate, and compete in the knowledge economy.* Jossey-Bass. Available: https://media.wiley.com/product_data/excerpt/3X/07879709/078797093X-196.pdf
7. Covey, S. R. (1989). *The 7 habits of highly effective people: Powerful lessons in personal change.* Simon & Schuster. Available: https://ati.dae.gov.in/ati12052021_1.pdf
8. Senge, P. M. (1990). *The fifth discipline: The art and practice of the learning organization.* Doubleday. Available: https://www.academia.edu/88173789/The_fifth_discipline_The_art_and_practice_of_the_learning_organization_by_Peter_Senge_New_York_Doubleday_Currency_1990

Be Curious

Mark Misquitta

Leadership Pearl

Curiosity has been my greatest strength when pursing professional development.

Scenario

In a world that constantly seeks increased value, being able to do things better than yesterday is gradually becoming the expectation as opposed to the exception. Being confined to learning via passive linear sources risks being left behind by our ever-evolving environment. Curiosity can certainly help with this. It fosters creativity by stimulating our imagination, sparking our interest and potentially fuelling our passion.

Discussion

Curiosity ignites the initial spark of interest that compels individuals to engage with new information. It is the desire to know more that drives learners to delve deeper into subjects and uncover knowledge they may have not otherwise found. When individuals are curious, they are more likely to pay attention, retain information and apply what they have learned. This intrinsic motivation to learn can lead to greater levels of achievement and a sense of fulfillment.

M. Misquitta (✉)
Strategic Finance and Governance, Monash Health, Melbourne, VIC, Australia

Department of Accounting, Monash University, Melbourne, VIC, Australia

In this regard, curiosity can boost the ability to learn and in turn enhance our professional performance. This learning mechanism helps us tackle challenges and find better solutions through questions, feedback and diverse perspectives. Curiosity makes us adaptable, open-minded and resilient, viewing changes as opportunities for growth. By exposing ourselves to different sources of inspiration and information, we can connect them to our work creatively, overcoming blocks and generating high-quality ideas.

Other Gems

Curiosity is a skill that we can cultivate and apply in our daily work. Here are some thoughts on how to help develop and practice curiosity in the workplace:

- *Set learning goals:* Identify what you want to learn, why you want to learn it and how you will learn it. Make a plan to achieve your learning goals and track your progress and results.
- *Seek new experiences*: Expose yourself to new and different situations, tasks, projects, or roles that challenge you and expand your comfort zone. Seek feedback and learn from your successes and failures.
- *Ask questions*: Ask open-ended, probing and clarifying questions that help you to understand the what, how and why of things. Ask questions that challenge your own and others' assumptions, opinions and perspectives.
- *Explore multiple sources*: Seek out and consume diverse and reliable sources of information such as books, articles, podcasts, videos, or people that relate to your work or interests. Compare and contrast different sources and evaluate their validity, relevance and usefulness.
- *Connect the dots*: Make connections between what you learn and what you do. Apply what you learn to your work and see how it improves your performance, creativity, or collaboration. Share what you learn with others and see how it benefits them or the team.
- *Be open-minded*: Be willing to change your mind, admit your mistakes and learn from others. Be receptive to new ideas, perspectives and feedback to evaluate them based on evidence and logic. Be flexible and adaptable to changes and uncertainties and see them as opportunities rather than threats.

The Art of Finance

Mark Misquitta

Leadership Pearl

The numbers are a picture, you are the artist.

Scenario

In organisations, financial numbers are often viewed as the definitive representation of an organisation's health and performance. These numbers, contained in balance sheets, income statements and cash flow reports, provide a snapshot of where the company stands at a particular moment in time. However, it is crucial to recognise that these numbers are merely a picture. A static image that captures the outcome of countless actions, decisions and strategies. The true creators of this picture are the people within the organisation. They are the artists who with their skills, creativity, and dedication, paint the financial landscape of the company.

Discussion

Financial numbers serve as a picture, offering a structured format to present the company's financial data. This picture, while informative, is devoid of the full truth. The picture can depict profits, losses, assets, and liabilities but it cannot convey the efforts, challenges, and innovations that contributed to these results.

M. Misquitta (✉)
Strategic Finance and Governance, Monash Health, Melbourne, VIC, Australia

Department of Accounting, Monash University, Melbourne, VIC, Australia

133

Just as a painting is brought to life by the artist's vision, technique, and passion, the financial picture of an organisation is crafted by its people. These individuals, with their diverse talents and commitment, are the true architects of financial success.

At the helm of the organisation are the strategic visionaries. The leaders who chart the course for the company. Their ability to anticipate trends, identify opportunities, and mitigate risks is crucial in shaping the financial outcomes. Their decisions, whether it is entering a new market or maintaining current services, have a profound impact on the financial picture.

Operational efficiency is another critical component of financial success. The managers and their teams, who oversee the day-to-day operations, ensure that the company runs smoothly and efficiently. Their ability to optimise processes, use resources wisely and strive for continuous improvement can result and contribute to a healthier bottom line.

Innovation is also critical for any organisation. Innovation is necessary to keep up with the times as it allows organisations to adapt to rapidly changing landscapes, technologies and stakeholders' preferences. Embracing innovation ensures that a company remains relevant and capable of meeting the evolving demands of the modern world.

Ultimately, the financial picture of an organisation is a collective masterpiece. It is created by the collaborative efforts of its people. Each department, each team, and each individual play a role in shaping this picture. Whether it be through strong leadership, well run operations and/or the ability to adapt and evolve, the numbers on the financial reports are the final strokes on the picture, representing the culmination of countless hours of hard work, dedication and ingenuity. Never losing sight of the organisation's purpose is the true key to creating a beautiful financial picture.

Part VI

Leadership in Crisis and Change

Communicating in a Crisis

Allen Cheng

Leadership Pearl

Communicating in a crisis is different to usual and needs to be timely and acknowledge the needs of your audience.

Situation

Crises can take many forms—the COVID-19 pandemic, an external Code Brown due to a natural disaster or an internal emergency. These have some similarities to medical emergencies in that are they are urgent situations where there is an acute threat, uncertainty, rapidly evolving information, and anxiety (in both healthcare staff and the public/patients) that can manifest in different ways.

Discussion

There are well established principles for managing incidents, including designating overall control, planning, collecting/analysing intelligence, providing public information, operations (tasking resources), investigation of the cause, logistics (procuring/acquiring resources) and finance [1]. In a smaller incident, these may be managed by a single person or small team; but major incidents may require whole teams for each function. Public communication can take a variety of forms from media statements to press conferences with journalists, to "town hall" meetings with staff, patients or affected communities.

A. Cheng (✉)
School of Clinical Sciences, Monash University, Melbourne, VIC, Australia

137

Peter Sandman, an expert in risk communication, frames the job of risk communication on a matrix of hazard and outrage.

(a) If the hazard is high but the outrage is low, the message is "watch out."
(b) If the hazard is low and outrage is high, the message is "calm down."
(c) In a crisis where there is a real hazard and everyone is aware, the job is about helping appropriately upset people cope with serious risks, with the message being "we'll get through this together."

In times of uncertainty, a universal need is to seek information from "someone in charge." If that's you as the most senior person available, below are a few things that might help.

- Sandman and Lanard have some useful principles [2, 3]:
    (i) Don't over-reassure.
    (ii) Proclaim uncertainty.
    (iii) Validate emotions.
    (iv) Give people things to do.
    (v) Admit and apologise for errors.
    (vi) Share dilemmas.
- You need to say what you know and what you don't. For what you don't know, it is helpful to say something about when you might know more (if you can) [4].
- You can't communicate frequently enough and if possible, make it predictable. For example, during the COVID pandemic, knowing press conferences were on at 11 am stopped a lot of questions at 10 am.
- Be empathetic and acknowledge that people are in different situations.
- No-one can be an expert in everything—develop a network of trusted informants and experts.

When you communicate, know your audience. The difficulty in public communications is that you often have multiple audiences—the public (via journalists), your colleagues and peers, and decision makers. One approach to this is to start simply then get more detailed and technical as you proceed.

Even though you may analyse a problem technically or statistically, you need to tell a story to convince others. Daniel Kahneman, the psychologist and Nobel Laureate, suggested "No one ever made a decision because of a number. They need a story" [5].

Other Gems

- Just as in a medical emergency where you fall back to first principles or a systems review, in a complex crisis, governance and process are things to fall back on when everything is chaotic.
- Some governance questions you may want to ask are:

    (i) Who needs to make a particular decision? Do you have the "authorising environment?"

    (ii) Can you define the question that needs to be answered and when?

    (iii) What information do you need?

    (iv) What are the alternatives (and pros and cons of each)?

    (v) What is the preferred option?

- Once you've made your decision, do your homework:
  - (i) What issues are others likely to have?
  - (ii) What are they likely to find acceptable?
  - (iii) Who do you need to consult with before it is announced?

If contacted by journalists,

- Are you allowed to speak to them? If so, make it clear who you are or are not representing. You may want to check with your hospital or university's public affairs unit.
- Are you the right person for them to speak to? (or the corollary, if you don't speak to them, are they just going to go to speak to someone less informed or sensible?) If you're not the right person, journalists will appreciate suggestions on who they should speak to.
- Prepare and plan- make a list of:
  - (i) The one message you want to convey (you will say this, no matter what question you're asked).
  - (ii) The 2–3 points you'd like to make if you have the time.
  - (iii) Answers to 2–3 awkward questions you might be asked.

References

1. Emergency Management Victoria. (2015). *Fundamentals of emergency management.* Victorian Government. Accessed at https://files-em.em.vic.gov.au/public/Doctrine/Fund/Fundamentals-EMC1.pdf. Accessed 5 June 2024.
2. Sandman, P. (2024). *Introduction to risk communication.* https://www.psandman.com/index-intro.htm. Accessed 5 June 2024.
3. Sandman, P., & Lanard, J. (2024). *Part 2: effective COVID-19 crisis communication. In COVID-19: the CIDRAP viewpoint.* Regents of the University of Minnesota, Minneapolis, United States, 2020. https://www.psandman.com/articles/Corona18.pdf. Accessed 5 June 2024.
4. Lanard, J. (2005). Talking to the public about a pandemic: Some applications of the WHO outbreak communication guidelines. *Yale Journal of Biology and Medicine, 78,* 369–376.
5. Lewis, M. (2016). *The undoing project: A friendship that changed our minds.* W.W. Norton & Co.

What Kind of Leader Are You? Be Every Kind

Sarah Lorentzen

Leadership Pearl

Different circumstances may call for a different style of leadership. Flex your leadership style to suit the situation you're in and the people you are leading.

Scenario

How many times in an interview have you been asked "what is your leadership style?" While it's true that to be an authentic leader, your style needs to be in-synch with your values and your personality, it is also vital that you can adapt your leadership to the situation. For example, I would say that overall, I'm a collaborative leader, but when it comes to getting my teenagers to pick up their shoes, left helpfully in the hallway, my leadership is far from collaborative (it's coercive at best, bordering on military junta). The point is you can't just be one style of leader. Well, you can, but it's not always going to work.

Discussion

There is much information available online and in the literature about leadership styles and how to identify the right one for you. However, according to psychologist Daniel Goleman, known for his work on emotional intelligence "being a great leader means recognising that different circumstances may call for different approaches" [1].

S. Lorentzen (✉)
Monash Health, Melbourne, VIC, Australia

In his 2000 Harvard Business Review (HBR) article, Goleman identified six distinct leadership styles that leaders can adopt, depending on the scenario and the needs of those they are leading. Rebecca Knight, in her 2024 HBR article, applied Goleman's work to today's business environment [2].

Coercive Leadership

This style entails demanding immediate compliance. Goleman believes that this is the least effective in most situations (hence the shoes that are still in the hallway). It is characterised by an authoritarian approach and a 'do what I say' attitude, and while this may achieve short term results and be useful in a crisis, long term this can be highly disempowering for teams. In my workplace, I saw this style of leadership emerge as we dealt with the COVID-19 pandemic. Decisions needed to be made quickly, within a clear chain of command, in a highly structured environment. This style of leadership has a role, but really only in a crisis.

Authoritative Leadership

This is about mobilising people toward a vision, by linking their work to a larger organisational strategy, and connecting their day-to-day role with a greater purpose. It is dependent on trusting the team to work towards a shared vision and purpose, with autonomy but within a clear framework. This style is associated with high employee engagement and job satisfaction. Goleman proposes that this is the most effective and inspiring style. In large, complex healthcare organisations, I can see how this would be an ideal style of leadership, but achieving this takes effort to (1) determine a shared vision and purpose that people want to sign up to, and (2) establishing the systems and processes to create autonomy and devolved decision-making. I'm all for this one, but it takes work.

Pacesetting Leadership

This involves expecting excellence and self-direction, holding yourself and others to high standards. While no-one would argue against striving for excellence, when the gap between the current state and excellence is wide or when this is applied in the wrong scenario, this style can result in employee stress and burnout. In public healthcare, the government sets clear targets for a range of performance measures, some of which are achievable, and others are simply not, due to a complex range of interconnecting variables and ever-increasing demand. An over-focus on achieving targets often comes at the expense of employee wellbeing and consumer experience. I work for an organisation whose strategic intent was 'the relentless pursuit of excellence.' On considering this statement in the development of the new strategic plan, it was almost unanimous to remove the concept of 'relentless', due to the association with employee fatigue.

Affiliative Leadership

This style centres around building strong emotional bonds, creating a sense of 'team' and fostering a positive and supportive workplace. It creates a sense of belonging, psychological safety to share ideas and opinions and a sense of working towards a common goal. This style recognises that employees have other things in their lives in addition to work, and that workplaces need to be safe places, both physically and emotionally. Post pandemic, and with the challenges faced globally in accessing a skilled workforce for healthcare, this style of leadership has never been more important. The establishment of wellbeing-related initiatives, roles and indeed whole departments, across multiple industries, including healthcare, is indicative of how important this is in a modern workplace.

Democratic Leadership

This involves creating consensus and empowering teams to have a role in decision-making. By consulting and listening to the opinions and concerns of a diverse range of stakeholders, individuals and teams will feel that their opinions are of value and their voices have been heard. This also frequently contributes to better solution design, with shared ownership, which can make the change management process significantly easier. Although, when decisions are time-critical or if the team is lacking the expertise to make a decision, it may not be the most effective style. However, used selectively, it can be a very powerful and popular style. This is often executed via the formation of committees, working groups, panels, councils and other forums where democratic leadership can be seen in action.

Coaching Leadership

This style is focused on individual growth and developing people for the future. It is more of a one-on-one leadership style and is related to the affiliative leadership style discussed above. Coaching is a leadership skill in itself and is highly reliant on a relationship of mutual trust between the coach and coachee. Coaching leadership can also be applied in multiple directions—coaching of a direct report (which one would argue is to be expected of a line manager), coaching of a peer or colleague (ideally at their request) or coaching of a manager (sometimes referred to as managing upwards). All directions require trust, consideration of advice being asked for and advice being given.

This list is not exhaustive and there are other styles of leadership quoted in the literature (for example, transactional, charismatic and laissez-faire, all to be used very selectively), but if you can utilise the above six styles in the right situation and with the right audience, you'll be on your way to being the full package leader, with a style to suit pretty much every scenario.

Other Gems

1. A relatively new and innovative style of leadership is *Transformational Leadership*. It's an inspirational style, that motivates people to bring their best. However, the transformational leader needs to have a high degree of trust of their staff, and also be trusted, and there is much work that needs to be done to get an organisation to a point of transformation. Sometimes, an organisation is not ready (or indeed willing) for a transformational leader.

References

1. Leadership That Gets Results. Daniel Goleman. Leadership That Gets Results (hbr.org)
2. 6 Common Leadership Styles – and How to Decide Which to Use When. Rebecca Knight. 6 Common Leadership Styles – and How to Decide Which to Use When (hbr.org)

Change Is as Good as a Holiday

Erwin Loh

Leadership Pearl

The leader needs to have the courage to make decisions in the middle of a crisis with limited information, while demonstrating authenticity that inspires others to follow during times of change.

Scenario

You are head of the General Medical unit, and your divisional director has tasked you to lead the hospital's response to a viral pandemic that threatens to overwhelm the resources and workforce of your organisation. You are initially overwhelmed by the enormous challenge, and struggle to know where to start. You are also faced by staff who are refusing to change how they do things. You remember the principles of adaptive leadership, understanding that you need to work with the frontline to come up with solutions to problems, and the steps required for effective change management. You follow these steps and are able to achieve some small wins. This leads to transformational change for the organisation that you successfully embed and sustain into the future.

E. Loh (✉)
Royal Australasian College of Medical Administrators, Melbourne, Australia

© The Author(s), under exclusive license to Springer Nature Singapore Pte Ltd. 2025   145
R. Junckerstorff, S. Baqar (eds.), *Leadership Pearls in Healthcare*,
https://doi.org/10.1007/978-981-96-4233-5_35

Discussion

The health system is traditionally slow to change and adopt new practices. One reason for this is that the health system is a complex adaptive system, where a perfect understanding of the individual parts does not automatically convey a perfect understanding of the whole system's behaviour [1]. Problems arising out of complex adaptive systems cannot be solved using technical solutions, but require adaptive leadership, an ability to work with experts from within the business to come up with adaptive solutions [2]. The leader who wants to find solutions for intractable problems in health needs to learn adaptive leadership techniques.

One constant in healthcare right now is that it is constantly changing. It is essential that the health leader has a framework for leading change, and one well-known change management model is Kotter's Eight Steps [3] (see Table 1).

Lastly, the change leader should be aware of the change curve model, based on the Kubler-Ross grief cycle [5]. Faced with change, people go through an initial phase of denial, before they transition to shock and confusion, and then anger and blame. This can lead to degraded performance. People can then move to a period of fear, anxiety and frustration as they are faced with learning new ways of doing things, before acceptance and optimism for the future. Change leaders need to

Table 1 Kotter's Eight Steps

Step 1	Establish a sense of urgency. In health, this should be straightforward, as the health system is moving from one crisis to another, whether it is lack of funding, workforce shortages or the challenge of rising chronic disease.
Step 2	Form a powerful guiding coalition. You need to engage clinical champions to support your change. A formal stakeholder analysis can be performed using a power-interest grid [4] to identify stakeholders with: (a) low interest and low power who need to be monitored (e.g. members of the general public). (b) high interest, but low power, who need to be kept informed (e.g. junior doctors for clinical projects). (c) high power, but low interest, who need to be kept satisfied (e.g. funders like the department of health). (d) high interest and high power who need to be actively engaged during the change process (e.g. clinicians for clinical projects).
Step 3	Develop a clear shared vision, something that is authentic and inspires others to follow you.
Step 4	Communicate the vision, with a clear communication strategy.
Step 5	Empower people to act on the vision, by providing them with an action plan.
Step 6	Plan for and create short term wins by creating obtainable targets in a pilot stage. Any early wins should be recognised and rewarded.
Step 7	Consolidate and build on the gains, by celebrating early success, expressing courage in the face of resistance, and maintaining the momentum for change.
Step 8	Institutionalise the change, by making it part of the culture of the organisation through embedding the change in new policies and procedures, remuneration structures, and training.

understand that these reactions are normal, and different people go through them at different speeds depending on how change ready they are.

Other Gems

- As a change agent in a healthcare setting, you can take an entrepreneurial approach to change by being an "intrapreneur" in that organisation.
- When following Kotter's Eight-Steps to change, do not skip a step or do things out of order—otherwise, the change may not be effective, and you may have to start over.
- It's important to understand that you need to be both an effective change manager and manage the change process according to time and budget, but you also need to be a change leader, and lead and inspire people through change through a compelling vision and influence.

References

1. Miller, J. H., & Page, S. E. (2007). *Complex adaptive systems: An introduction to computational models of social life*. Princeton University Press.
2. Kuluski, K., Reid, R. J., & Baker, G. R. (2021, April). Applying the principles of adaptive leadership to person-centred care for people with complex care needs: Considerations for care providers, patients, caregivers and organizations. *Health Expect., 24*(2), 175–181.
3. Kotter, J. P. (1996). *Leading change*. Harvard Business School Press.
4. Mendelow, A. (1991, December 7–9). *Stakeholder mapping*. In Proceedings of the 2nd International conference on information systems.
5. Kessler, E., & Kubler-Ross, D. (2014). *On grief and grieving*. Simon & Schuster.

Be Yourself

Brett Sutton

Leadership Pearl

There is never a more important time to be one's true self than during a crisis.

Scenario

During a crisis or pandemic, there is enormous uncertainty, anxiety, and a need for building of trust. For COVID-19, this was compounded by the most severe and consequential pandemic for a century; a new pandemic virus (SARS-CoV-2); and intense mainstream and social media cycles on a background of ideological polarisation. Leaders can be tempted to speak only to certainties and to focus on consistency of messaging, even as different evidence emerges, and new challenges and circumstances unfold. They may be motivated to minimise the unknown, or to shield the public from complex or troubling data. They're unlikely to admit mistakes or to apologise for misplaced decisions. This may be ultimately well-meaning, but it fails to engender the very trust of community that is being sought.

Discussion

Courageous leadership requires us to be honest, not over-reassuring; to be upfront about uncertainty; to validate people's emotions and to reveal our own struggles and dilemmas [1]. The tendency to over-reassure comes from the misapprehension that communities can't appraise risk; that they'll panic or over-react. The reality is that

---

B. Sutton (✉)
Melbourne, VIC, Australia

panic is extremely rare and that the term is often applied to what might more rightly be called an adjustment reaction. Communities need the time and opportunity to absorb the new reality facing them; to grieve; and to emotionally adjust to the uncertainty and challenge of what they're facing or might face.

A similar dynamic applies to underplaying uncertainty. It arises from the mistaken belief that a community will be more reassured by static, ruthlessly consistent messaging. The only problem with that—and it's a big problem—is that pandemics and other crises are not static, and the disconnect between messaging and reality becomes ever more stark. People will be more reassured by a leader who reflects a changing reality, new insights or realisations than one who stubbornly insists that what people come to experience and understand is somehow a fantasy.

The issue of 'bringing your authentic self' has perhaps been overused in leadership narratives, but it's an inescapable necessity in a crisis. Many, many community members are struggling themselves. They might be suffering in myriad ways – with anxiety or fear, with sadness, loneliness or grieving. They want that to be acknowledged, explicitly and with empathy. They also want to know that they're not alone in their struggles and that the crisis leadership team is right alongside them. So, revealing your own battles and vulnerabilities is crucial for many reasons. It makes obvious your empathy and your recognition of the communal struggle—"We're all in this together." It also 'gives permission' to others to reach out for help themselves—"If they can do it, then so can I." And, of course, it helps you as a leader to get through what is likely to be the most challenging of life circumstances. It is amazing how others can respond to seeing a leader reveal themselves in such a way.

Other Gems

1. In a crisis, there are only bad choices. Our obligation is to seek out and commit to the least worst choice.
2. Doing nothing is also an action. Don't wait for perfect information or absolute clarity. Act fast if consequences are playing out in front of you.
3. We will all make mistakes. Leadership is in owning them and apologising for them.

Reference

1. Sandman, P., & Lanard, J. (2020, May 6). *COVID-19: The CIDRAP viewpoint. Part 2: Effective COVID-19 crisis communication.*

Part VII

Work-Life Balance

Prioritise Self-Care to Give Yourself the Best Chance to Succeed

Anjali Dhulia

Leadership Pearl

Looking after our own physical, emotional, and mental health is the first step towards fulfilling our personal and professional goals.

Scenario

James was in his final year of speciality training. His exams were looming, he had just come off a week of night shifts, and had picked up a couple of locum shifts on his days off. At home, his wife was in the final weeks of a difficult pregnancy, expecting their first child. Being a devoted husband, James took on most of the housework. He felt exhausted and irritable. He was short with his juniors and noticed himself taking shortcuts with his work. A consultant noticed that James was not his usual sharp and organised self and seemed to be struggling with his workload. After the ward round, the consultant took him aside for a coffee and asked him if he was okay. This kind gesture helped James open up about his situation and ask for help. The consultant helped him get a couple of days off, advised him to organise help at home if possible and cautioned against taking on extra work at this time. They advised him to make self-care a priority and look after his physical, emotional, and mental health, as only then would he be able to fulfil his personal and professional goals successfully.

A. Dhulia (✉)
Monash Health, Melbourne, VIC, Australia

Discussion

Medical training years are probably the most challenging time in a doctor's career. Balancing work and study, moving jobs every year, possibly a young family, increasing financial responsibilities, social expectations of success are just some of the issues that young doctors grapple with. At such a time, it is critical that we set ourselves up for success by ensuring we are in the best possible state of fitness to meet these challenges without falling apart.

In his book, *Effortless*, Greg McKeown describes the "Effortless State" as a state when we are physically rested, emotionally unburdened, and mentally energised [1]. According to McKeown, in this state, one is completely aware, alert, present, attentive, and focused on what's important in this moment and able to focus on what matters most with ease. We are able to think clearly, prioritise our actions, problem-solve and meet our own expectations of ourselves.

Medical training is demanding and to meet these demands, our own health must remain at the top of our to-do list. We must ensure we make time for sleep, rest, nutrition, exercise, relaxation, recreation, time with loved ones, social connections, personal administration, medical appointments and many other responsibilities towards our own health and wellbeing. Otherwise, we are at risk of reaching a state of physical, emotional, and mental exhaustion that may prevent us from realising our goals and our full potential.

Other Gems

1. Ask yourself everyday: Am I feeling good and functioning well? If not, explore why and address the cause.
2. Look out for your colleagues and make it a point to ask if they are okay.
3. Sometimes it is prudent to intentionally postpone some of our goals to make time and space for others. In a career spanning 40–50 years, there will be time for everything.

Reference

1. McKeown, G. (2021). *Effortless: Make it easier to do what matters*. Penguin Random House, UK.

You Are More Than Your Work

Erwin Loh

Leadership Pearl

The trick to work-life balance is to stop believing that they are dichotomous concepts that need balancing but accepting that we are holistic beings that are mature enough to be able to integrate both into our identities without sacrificing our own well-being and our relationships.

Scenario

You are on-call for your clinical unit and you realise that tonight is also your child's school play. You want to attend the school play, but you know you are likely going to get calls during that time. You also know that you have a long list of emails that you need to address, and even though it's dinner time with the family, you are tempted to check your mobile device to answer a few of the urgent emails. You are worried that you have no work-life balance as there is a sense of dread that your work is seeping into your home life. You recalibrate your thinking and reframe your perspective. You understand that work and life separation is artificial. You prioritise your family time according to your personal values, are mindful and present when with your loved ones, and set time aside when you can concentrate on work matters. You decide to check your emails after dinner, and attend your child's play, letting work know that during that hour you will not be contactable, but will respond right after.

E. Loh (✉)
Royal Australasian College of Medical Administrators, Melbourne, Australia

Discussion

People often refer to work-life balance as though work and personal life are separate mutually exclusive components that somehow need to be kept in balance, suggesting an almost fifty-fifty split to keep each of them equal. However, human beings wear multiple hats at the same time—we can be a worker, parent, significant other, and sibling all at once. It is important that we do not create a single personal identity based on a single role, as that role can take over a person's sense of being—this is known as "enmeshment" [1].

Rather, it is more helpful to see our personal identities as integrating the different roles we have and all the aspects of our lives, including our work, studies, family, hobbies, and other interests. In this way, we invest time and effort not just in our work at the expense of the other parts of our lives, but we ensure that we spend time investing in our other roles, as they are all inter-connected and part of us. For example, a healthy family life usually leads to a healthy work life [2].

Nevertheless, we can be faced with conflicting requests for our focus when our different roles request our attention at the same time. At that point, we need to prioritise our time according to what is important versus what is urgent. It becomes less an issue of balancing between priorities, and more about "resource allocation" based on your values—deciding what is important, and allocating time and focus to those first as a priority [3]. It is best to decide on your personal priorities in a planned way before you are faced with having to make difficult decisions, so that when decisions have to be made, it becomes an easier process.

It is also important that when you do make a decision to do something—for example, spend time with family—that you are present not just physically, but emotionally and mentally as well. In other words, practice mindfulness when you are engaging in a task based on the role you are playing at the time. Being mindful while spending time with family or doing things you enjoy means you are not distracted by work, but are also present for those you are with. Mindfulness when engaging in such tasks improves overall life satisfaction [4].

One method to effectively transition from different roles, situations or environments, such as being busy at work to being a parent at home, is called "The Third Space" [5]. When moving from the "First Space" to the "Second Space", effective leaders transition through the "Third Space"—basically a time when you can Reflect ("How do I interpret what just happened to me?"), Rest ("Can I be still and present?") and Reset ("How will I 'show up'?"). This is an effective method to ensure that you do not carry burdens and emotions from a previous meeting to a new one, or from work to the home.

Other Gems

1. It's okay to check work emails at home if you have purposefully set aside time to do this, you are not doing it while spending time with family, and you ensure that you have not resourced too much time to doing it at the expense of other things that may be more important.
2. You are more than your work—but work is part of you. Therefore, ensure your personal identity is properly integrated so that no one part of your life becomes your full identity as a person.
3. In the end, everyone is different. Discover your own path to ensure you live a fulfilled and satisfied life, that feels not just balanced, but meaningful.

References

1. Koretz, J. (2019, December). What happens when your career becomes your whole identity. *Harvard Business Review.*
2. Levterova, D. (2013 June). *Personal identity in the balance between work and family.* In CBU international conference proceedings (Vol. 1, pp. 247–253).
3. Grawitch, M. J., Barber, L. K., & Justice, L. (2010, June). Rethinking the work–life interface: It's not about balance, it's about resource allocation. *Applied Psychology: Health and Well-Being, 2,* 127–159.
4. Althammer, S. E., Reis, D., van der Beek, S., Beck, L., & Michel, A. (2021). A mindfulness intervention promoting work–life balance: How segmentation preference affects changes in detachment, well-being, and work–life balance. *J Occup Organ Psychol, 94,* 282–308.
5. Fraser, A. (2012). *The third space.* William Heinemann.

Non-Binary Approaches to Enable a Flexible Work-Life Rhythm

Rhonda Wilson, Barbora de Courten, and Karen Livesay

Leadership Pearl

Work-life balance is traditionally presented as a binary concept. It suggests that work and life are expected to have equal or calibrated weighting. In the real-world however, lives pivot across change, disruptions and uncertainties which can upset the 'equilibrium.' This can lead to personal stress, suboptimal coping or failure. In the context of prolonged and/or unpredictable disruptions, personal resilience reservoirs can quickly deplete. A more flexible acknowledgement of the continuum of life rhythms may lead to contextually sustainable and resilient approaches for workers and teams.

Scenario

Emma is a 45-year-old clinical nurse consultant in a specialist early psychosis clinic, balancing responsibilities across clinical practice, team education, research, budget management, and patient care transitions. Her role spans child, adolescent and adult mental health services, in acute and community settings.

R. Wilson · K. Livesay
School of Health & Biomedical Sciences, STEM College, RMIT University, Melbourne, VIC, Australia

B. de Courten (✉)
School of Health & Biomedical Sciences, STEM College, RMIT University, Melbourne, VIC, Australia

Department of General Medicine, Monash Health, Melbourne, VIC, Australia

At home, Emma is a mother of three (ages 7–12) and shares domestic and parenting responsibilities with her partner, a busy police officer. Both have demanding careers, facing intermittent periods of intense work and stress. Additionally, Emma manages her chronic migraine condition and is peri-menopausal.

Despite the challenges, Emma practices dadirri self-care, engages in clinical supervision [1], and values a flexible approach that allows her to respond to the fluctuating demands of her professional and personal life. She feels most fulfilled when she has the autonomy and self-agency to work to her strengths that accommodates her unique, occasionally disruptive, life rhythms.

Discussion

The traditional work-life balance model is limited in that it relies on notions of paternalistic self-efficacy with an absence of a buffer margin, especially for women. Traditional work-life balance models have privileged 'breadwinner' males and perpetuated oppressive female 'carer' roles, rather than dual-earner families [2]. This traditional legacy continues to propagate disparity in the health workforce in achieving equality in work-life balance.

Managers in the health professions are naturally focussed on professional work objectives and are not always mindful of supporting models that provide the necessary freedom, flexibility and agility required to manage the fluctuating demands of both personal and professional life. This can leave team members feeling disenfranchised, fatigued and unhappy.

Work-life balance places the problem of balance solely with the individual. Using a feminist standpoint theoretical lens, it is possible to highlight some emancipatory responses to managing workplace stressors, particularly for women who make up a large segment of the health workforce [3].

Work-Life Rhythm Continuum

An effective approach to occasional disruptive life imbalances is to embrace a non-binary, strength-based perspective. This approach incorporates a range of contextually situated cognitive, emotional, and social intelligence to maximise flexibility and self-determined solutions [4]. This allows for greater flexibility and responsiveness to the dynamic nature of life and work rhythms. It enables people to move fluidly and contextually between periods of high intensity and relaxation, accommodating the peaks (orderliness) and troughs (disruptions) of rhythms in both work and life.

Work-life balance narratives often align with resilience but can unfairly shift responsibility onto workers. No amount of resilience or self-care can offset unreasonable workloads, leading to burnout and job dissatisfaction [4, 5]. Managers should empower team members to establish personalised work-life rhythms, respecting their full life demands. Open communication and tools to decline tasks when necessary, can prevent overwork. Flexibility and recognising work as part of a broader life rhythm encourages self-directed time management and self-efficacy and appropriate delegation when needed [5].

Resilience

Resilience involves adapting to personal challenges through flexible cognitive, emotional, and behavioural adjustments [4]. Early views of resilience were static, focusing on balancing risk and protective factors, expecting individuals to manage work-life stress through self-care [4]. This approach positions complex personal circumstances as risks to be balanced with routines, selfcare, and supervision. However, it unfairly places blame on individuals when they struggle, ignoring the complexity of their situations. It emphasises bouncing back from disruptions without improving long-term capacity or strength, leading to self-blame and stigma for failing to maintain work-life balance.

Strategies to Promote a Healthy Work-Life Rhythm: Individual and Organisational Shared Responsibility

Promoting resilience in healthcare requires both individual strategies, such as emotional intelligence and self-efficacy, and organisational support through leadership and workplace interventions [4].

1. On an individual level, effective strategies may include maintaining effective and familiar work-life routines, organising activities mindfully, and using personal attributes such as self-determination, self-reliance, passion, interest, positive thinking, and emotional intelligence to boost self-efficacy [6].
2. Organisational strategies should focus on providing both formal and informal support services, fostering empathetic and emotionally intelligent management and leadership, open and non-judgemental communication, flexibility and encouraging role modelling [6].

Tips for Managers to Promote Health Professionals' Intention to Stay at Work and Buffer the Intention to Leave Early

1. **Dadirri:** In the Australian context, Aboriginal Elders have gifted the culturally rich life-work-rhythm traditional knowledge of Dadirri to assist people to work with the ebbs and flows of life. Central to the practice of Dadirri is deep and still inner listening. This is not so much reflecting or thinking, but rather an 'in the moment' stillness to listen to self within the ecological context one is situated within. It is a preparedness to move with the seasons and episodes of work and life that are inherent in our lives. Dadirri is a form of mindfulness that supports

coping and sustains resilience by practicing still inner listening and quiet strong awareness [7].

2. **Address workload/caseload and job strain**: To enhance the likelihood of employees staying at work, especially those dealing with stress or depression, it is important to limit excessive workloads/ caseloads, minimise overtime, implement flexible rostering, and reduce job strain [5].

3. **Facilitate supportive work environments**: Ensure that team members have meaningful social connections and support within the workplace. Strong social support is important for promoting emotional intelligence and maintaining engagement and productivity [5]. Eliminate taboo and stigma to support well-being. For example, in Emma's case as she copes with perimenopause and migraine without shame [8].

4. **Implement emotionally and culturally safe workplaces**: Enhance positive sentiment in the workplace. For example, intentional acts of kindness and taking time to say thank you; authentically enquire about the well-being of colleagues; expressions of empathy and gratitude; recognition of culturally meaningful holidays and celebrations.

5. **Encourage autonomy**: Accommodate self-determination and a degree of control over work tasks and environment. This autonomy helps people to manage stress and maintain a positive work experience [5].

6. **Monitor and adjust workload**: Regularly evaluate and reasonably adjust employees' workloads to ensure they are manageable. This helps prevent overburdening and supports mental health [4, 5].

7. **Promote active coping**: Create opportunities for employees such as Emma to engage in active coping strategies. This might include flexibility in work arrangements, modifiable environments, or resources for mental health, chronic conditions or menopause support [5, 8, 9].

8. **Enhance overall well-being**: Support initiatives that improve employees' health, cognitive functioning, and work performance. Improved well-being can positively impact their ability to stay at work [5].

9. **Leverage positive feedback loops**: Recognise that improving symptom management can have cascading benefits. For instance, addressing mental health vulnerabilities early can lead to improved performance and further support an intention to remain in the workforce [5].

10. **Active communication**: Listen carefully, with respect. Apply strategies such as ISBAR (Introduction; Situation; Background; Assessment; Recommendation) to streamline context-based efficiency in communication [10].

Conclusion

Emma's story illustrates the complex real-world work and life contexts that many health professionals encounter. It demonstrates the need for solutions that straddle a continuum of experiences and are not solely tied to binary explanations. Adopting a work-life rhythm approach assists in retaining a strong and resilient health workforce while mitigating fatigue or burnout that can lead to an intention to leave work.

References

1. White, E., & Winstanley, J. (2011). Clinical supervision for mental health professionals: The evidence base. *Social Work & Social Sciences Review, 14*(3), 77–94.
2. Pircher, B., De La Porte, C., & Szelewa, D. (2024). Actors, costs and values: The implementation of the work-life balance directive. *West European Politics, 47*(3), 543–568.
3. Ashton, N. A., & Mckenna, R. (2020). Situating feminist epistemology. *Episteme, 17*(1), 28–47.
4. Margetts, J., Hazelton, M., Santangelo, P., Yorke, J., & Wilson, R. l. (2024). Measurement of psychological resilience to support therapy interventions for clients in the clinical mental healthcare setting: A scoping review. *International Journal of Mental Health Nursing.*
5. van Hees, S. G., et al. (2022). Towards a better understanding of work participation among employees with common mental health problems: A systematic realist review. *Scandinavian Journal of Work, Environment & Health, 48*(3), 173–189.
6. Badu, E., et al. (2020). Workplace stress and resilience in the Australian nursing workforce: A comprehensive integrative review. *International Journal of Mental Health Nursing, 29*(1), 5–34.
7. Ungunmerr, M.-R. (1988). *Dadirri: Inner deep listening and quiet still awareness.* https://www.miriamrosefoundation.org.au/about-dadirri
8. Cronin, C., Hungerford, C., & Wilson, R. L. (2021). Using digital health technologies to manage the psychosocial symptoms of menopause in the workplace: A narrative literature review. *Issues in Mental Health Nursing, 42*(6), 541–548.
9. Cronin, C., et al. (2024). Menopause at work – An organisation-based case study. *Nursing Open, 11*(1).
10. Burgess, A., et al. (2020). Teaching clinical handover with ISBAR. *BMC Medical Education, 20*(S2).

Empathic Leadership: Supporting Staff in High-Stress Environments

Barbora de Courten and Karen Livesay

Leadership Pearl

Leaders work empathically with staff that report to them. Leaders monitor their staff's workload, help them prioritise their work, and provide additional resources when and where needed. Leaders create a safe space to discuss workload and give agency to staff to raise concerns if they arise.

Scenario

Dr. AC began his rotation as a medical registrar at a major metropolitan hospital in Melbourne, following in the footsteps of his parents, both general physicians. From the outset, he managed a heavy workload, caring for 25–27 patients daily and admitting 5–7 new patients each day. His days often extended well past his scheduled hours, with ward rounds sometimes lasting until 7pm. He was frequently only getting home after 8pm.

Three months into his role, Dr. AC was still staying at work much longer than his rostered hours. He frequently skipped lunch or ate while reviewing results. His previously regular gym visits ceased due to exhaustion. His preparation for his

B. de Courten (✉)
School of Health & Biomedical Sciences, STEM College, RMIT University,
Melbourne, VIC, Australia

Department of General Medicine, Monash Health, Melbourne, VIC, Australia

K. Livesay
School of Health & Biomedical Sciences, STEM College, RMIT University,
Melbourne, VIC, Australia

specialist exams was also time-consuming, leaving little room for relaxation or socialising. The medical team often operated short-staffed, or with a steady stream of locum doctors unfamiliar with the patients, adding to Dr. AC's stress. The increasing stress levels began to affect Dr. AC's sleep, concentration, and memory. Despite his struggles, he hesitated to discuss his workload with his consultant, influenced by stories of the long hours his parents and other senior doctors endured in the past. His chronic fatigue led to irritability and headaches, culminating in a critical error where he prescribed the wrong medication dose. This incident prompted Dr. AC to finally voice his concerns about his workload and fatigue to his consultant.

Discussion

Dr. AC's experience as a medical registrar underscores the critical role that effective leadership plays in supporting team members, particularly in high-stress environments. His journey highlights several areas where managerial support could have made a significant difference.

Proactive Communication and Support

Managers (in this case a consultant or a head of the unit) should foster an environment where open communication is encouraged and supported. According to Groysberg and Slind [1], leadership should be more conversational rather than directive. If Dr. AC's consultant had established regular check-ins and created a safe space for discussing workload and stress, Dr. AC may have felt more comfortable voicing his concerns earlier. Proactive communication can help identify issues before they escalate. An archaic belief in healthcare often expressed as "we had to do it, so why can't you?" reflects a mindset that perpetuates unnecessary hardship and burnout among doctors. This outdated perspective fails to recognise the importance of evolving work environments to prioritise well-being and sustainable practices for current and future healthcare professionals.

Providing Adequate Resources and Staffing

Ensuring that a team is adequately staffed and supported is crucial. In Dr. AC's case, consistent understaffing and the reliance on unfamiliar cover doctors added to his stress. The head of the unit should prioritise securing reliable staffing solutions and providing resources that enable team members to perform their duties effectively without being overburdened. However, it is important to recognise that this can be challenging given fiscal constraints and the increasing difficulty in finding junior doctors due to burnout and moral injury.

Encouraging Work-Life Balance

Managers should actively promote work-life balance and self-care among their team members [2]. Coaching leaders to ask the right questions about their colleagues' motivations and obstacles can enhance their decision-making skills. Dr. AC's consultant could have encouraged him to take regular breaks, prioritise his well-being, and seek help when needed. By fostering a culture that values self-care, managers can help prevent burnout and maintain team morale.

Conclusion

Effective leadership in high-stress environments involves proactive communication, adequate resource allocation, and promoting work-life balance. By supporting team members, managers can create a more resilient and productive workforce.

References

1. Groysberg, B., & Slind, M. (2012). Leadership is a conversation. *Harvard Business Review*.
2. Schwartz, T. (2022). To coach leaders, ask the right questions. *Harvard Business Review*.

Leading at Work. Leading Outside Work. Leading ALL THE TIME. Is Leadership Fatigue a Thing?

Sarah Lorentzen

Leadership Pearl

Leadership skills are completely transferable, not only between jobs but also between your professional and your personal life. This can be really useful, but leadership fatigue is a real thing.

Scenario

I'm a leader at work. I lead people, I lead projects, I spend a lot of my time 'leading.' And so it's pretty natural that outside work, I gravitate towards leadership roles. I enjoy a pretty hectic schedule of extra-curricular activities—masters athletics, choir, fitness teaching—and invariably I'm asked to take on leadership roles (my husband has now put a cap on the number of committees I can be on). Plus I have a leadership role at home—I need to lead my two teenagers (they REALLY enjoy that) and sometimes I need to lead my husband (he PARTICULARLY enjoys that—"can you please stop project managing me"). But sometimes I feel tired of being a leader – it would be so nice just to be a follower for once! Maybe what I'm feeling is leadership fatigue.

S. Lorentzen (✉)
Monash Health, Melbourne, VIC, Australia

169

Discussion

Leadership fatigue occurs when the burden of leadership overtakes a leader's effectiveness. It can cause a leader to struggle to stay motivated, passionate or energetic and they may find it difficult to motivate, guide or encourage team members. It can begin with a sense of literal fatigue and then progress to feelings of stagnation, lack of purpose, work or obligation avoidance, disconnection and resentment. This ultimately has negative consequences for the individual as a leader, and for the organisation or team they are leading.

The statistics from a report examining responses from over 2000 human resources professionals and close to 16,000 leaders are sobering:

1. 60% of leaders reported feeling 'used up' at the end of their workday [1].
2. 76% felt 'overwhelmed' with managing their people [1].
3. Amongst senior leaders, 50% of women and 40% of men felt 'burned out' and this gap between the genders is getting wider [2].

However, there are several ways to recognise and overcome leadership fatigue:

1. *Be aware of your emotions*—do things feel 'normal' to you? Certainly, a little bit of stress can be a helpful motivator to get things done, but going over that tipping point of being overly stressed can have really detrimental effects. Take your self-analysis beyond 'stressed.' What are the emotions you are experiencing, and what are the triggers? It might help to write it down in a diary, so you can see if there is a pattern. Sometimes just understanding why things are happening or why you are feeling the way you are gives you the power to start thinking about the solution.
2. *Be clear about your purpose*—rather helpfully, at work your purpose is often documented in your position description, in your performance review or in your performance indicators. Going back to organisation or team priorities can also be a helpful exercise to re-prioritise your effort. Outside of work, sometimes the purpose of why we get involved in things can be less clear. Or it starts one way (I'd like to do some athletics) and then becomes something else (I've just agreed to be the club president, well, because everyone said I'd be good at it, and they will help, and no-one else wants to do it). It's ok just to turn up sometimes—most other people do that!
3. *Know your limits*—everyone has a point where they reach saturation, where they really can't take on any more without negative consequence. In our post-pandemic world, where the boundaries between our work and our home lives are far more blurred, this can be a hard balance to find. It's also useful to understand the limits of others, so that you aren't piling more work onto an already overworked employee, or you aren't asking kids to do extra chores when maybe they have a pile of assignments due. Knowing your limits and the limits of others is key.

4. ***Ask for help***—sometimes leaders feel that they need to do everything themselves (I'm a bit of a control freak, so I frequently feel this way). But leadership is a team sport, and sometimes great leadership is showing vulnerability and admitting when things are too much or you're dropping the ball. If a colleague offers to help, this might be a sign that they have noticed that you've got too much on your plate. Don't dismiss those offers. You might need to renegotiate timelines with those you are delivering to, delegate work to others or simply de-prioritise something. The same goes for your personal life. Saying no to a child, a partner, a social event, a(nother) committee is at times easier said than done for fear of disappointing those you care about or the risk of FOMO, but if you've got the feeling that the next commitment is too much, it probably is.

5. ***Don't let good be the enemy of great***—with the pace of change in healthcare and high expectations of leaders, perfection is a pretty high bar, and not always realistic to achieve. Sometimes close enough is good enough.

Other Gems

1. Just because you are a leader (and perhaps a really good leader), you don't need to be the one to lead all the time. Providing leadership opportunities to others or indeed just being one of the team is a great opportunity for you to remember what it's like to support a leader and can also help with managing leadership fatigue.

2. Your own health and wellbeing are paramount. Be conscious and intentional about how you manage your own wellbeing. All the usual stuff—eat well, get enough sleep and exercise—but also having meaningful relationships with people outside of work, hobbies and extra-curricular activities and taking time to switch off.

References

1. Global Leadership Forecast. (2021). *Development Dimensions International.*
2. The state of burnout for women in the workplace (podcast). McKinsey, Jan 4, 2022.

Love Your Life

Mark Misquitta

Leadership Pearl

You can't always assume you will be passionate about your job, but loving your life can provide motivation that is valuable for prosperity at work.

Scenario

"Find a job you are passionate about and you'll never work a day in your life." This famous phrase sounds good in theory, however, can be quite elusive to achieve. Just because we may work in jobs that aren't in our top things to do at any given moment does not mean we can't be captivated, challenged and motivated to succeed in them. The drive to succeed and perform can be derived from the role work plays in our lives. You may have to accept that you are good at things you don't love but they allow you to acquire and divert resources to the things you do.

Discussion

One way to look at work is as an exchange. One where we trade our time for resources, typically money. Those resources are then directed to priorities we have, both needs and wants.

Technically it is our needs (things required for basic human survival) rather than wants that should drive our desire and enthusiasm for our work. However, for those

M. Misquitta (✉)
Strategic Finance and Governance, Monash Health, Melbourne, VIC, Australia

Department of Accounting, Monash University, Melbourne, VIC, Australia

© The Author(s), under exclusive license to Springer Nature Singapore Pte Ltd. 2025   173
R. Junckerstorff, S. Baqar (eds.), *Leadership Pearls in Healthcare*,
https://doi.org/10.1007/978-981-96-4233-5_42

of us who live in the developed world, this is often not a compelling enough reason, as our needs will generally be met whether it be through our own efforts or those of the system around us.

In reality, it is our wants that can evoke the primal sense of pursuit and the attainment of that which we desire. This can come in many forms and can include things such as holidays, time with our families, and material possessions. It is through our wants that we can find the drive to propel us forward in our working lives.

Striving for something that provides significant meaning or joy to you, might just be everything you need to thrive in what may be an inherently unfulfilling professional circumstance.

We also must be clear on whether we are good at what we do. Having clarity allows us to find peace in our professional choices. If we are poor at something and don't enjoy it, one must ask why would we endure it? Success at work can directly correlate with our passions outside of work and can provide us with the resources to access the experiences we desire.

With this mentality we can find reassurance that our work is only one piece of the life we love. Loving your life may allow you to see that it is the sum of all parts that enable you to enjoy it. This gives real purpose to the work you do.

Other Gems

1. It is often said that being happy is a choice. If that is true, it infers that deliberate choices (physical, mental or emotional) can shape your outlook. Be deliberate about your work and understand its place in your life.

Resilience and Self-Compassion

Eugine Yafele

Leadership Pearl

Resilience and self-compassion are not a destination, they are a work in progress that requires regular and consistent practice.

Scenario

I usually have a busy day of scheduled meetings and often go to different locations to address a diverse audience on a wide range of issues. On this day, I was scheduled to meet with governors of the health service regarding proposed changes to the provision of community hospital services that would result in ward closures. I had spent what I thought was a considerable amount of time in stakeholder groups, talking about the proposed changes. I anticipated debate and passionate exchanges of ideas but expected the governors to be supportive of the proposal albeit with reservations.

The meeting was difficult and there was a sense of betrayal and considerable challenge from the governors. I felt under pressure to 'land the deal' and began to question how well I had laid the ground before the meeting. My internal monologue was self-critical and unkind and diminished all that I had done. In that moment, I felt like a failure, my demeanour reflected that, and it compromised my ability to listen and understand whilst dialling up my intention to hear and respond.

As the quality of discussion in the meeting deteriorated (primarily because of how I was showing up), I checked in with myself—I recognised the self-sabotage at play caused by my lack of self-compassion. This was driving my behaviour and

E. Yafele (✉)
Monash Health, Melbourne, Australia

affecting the tempo of the meeting. I reset mentally and shared with the governors that my fight response was not appropriate as I was clearly not valuing their feedback. I felt under pressure and asked for a break for us to reset.

I came back to the meeting and detailed the changes that had been made on the back of feedback received and the progress we had made. I also however, conceded that the proposed changes represented a real threat to the community and that more work was needed before we could arrive at an agreed position. After more engagement and further refinement of the plans, the governors gave their support, and the change was implemented.

Discussion

I often talk to colleagues about self-compassion as a necessary first step to compassionate leadership, less as an instruction but as a note to self! This is because as a fully paid-up member of the compassionate leadership faithful, there are times that I still struggle to be compassionate to myself. In my experience, self-compassion has a profound impact on personal resilience and both attributes influence how we show up as leaders.

I am very intentional about my self-check-in. This practice takes many forms; looking at the week ahead as I review the diary, as I prepare for engagements or when I encounter challenges in my day as well as reflecting on the meeting, day or week. This practice allows me to understand what I have going on, what my priorities are and how I am feeling about it all. This also gives me time and space to be honest about the things on my list and in my head that need my attention.

It also gives me the opportunity to manage expectations of self, helps me avoid pursuing perfection and grounds me in the reality of what it will take to get through the meeting, conversation, day or whatever is ahead of me. This is particularly important when I am feeling under pressure and have complex and challenging issues to deal with, which for most leaders is the reality of most days in the job!

Self-compassion tempers my tendency to be hard on myself when things do not go as I would have hoped. This is also where my resilience is found. When faced with tough issues that have no simple solutions, the ability to ground myself in the reality of what I have been able to do, the people I can turn to, the agency I have, all build my resilience. I may not have done something before; however, I have over time, developed the skills, tools and patience to work my way through it.

The challenge remains how I (and indeed all leaders) make the time in a busy job and life to pause, reflect and re-energise. This is an act of self-compassion that takes intention, regular practice and dedication. It requires the humility to accept that I will not get it done as often as I would like and to the standard I expect and demand of myself, but I persist, and go at it again and again. In doing so, I build resilience and have more opportunity to be the best version of myself to lead with authenticity, compassion, and bravery.

Presence Is Powerful

Chris Gartside

Leadership Pearl

Find time and ways to be present and ensure that this is meaningful. It allows you as a leader to understand the system, people, and challenges, and gives you credibility when posing questions and/or proposing change.

Scenario

A hospital department leader notices a decline in operational performance, team morale and an increase in staff turnover. The department leader finds themselves able to approach and speak to key persons, spend more time on the floor, interact with staff, and observe daily operations. This presence allows for participation in morning rounds, attendance at team meetings, and taking time to speak with staff individually. By being present, the department leader gains and builds credibility and relationships, ensuring a deeper understanding of the issues faced by the team. As a result, they identify several areas needing improvement. Their presence not only boosts staff morale but also lends credibility to the department leader's subsequent proposals for change.

C. Gartside (✉)
Emergency Services and Access Division, Northern Health, Melbourne, VIC, Australia

Discussion

In leadership, presence is a powerful tool that goes beyond merely being physically available. It involves active engagement and meaningful interaction with team members. When leaders make a conscious effort to be present, they gain invaluable insights into the workings of their team and organisation. This understanding is crucial for identifying challenges, fostering a supportive environment, and implementing effective changes [1, 2].

Leadership presence can be broken down into several key components.

First, it involves *physical presence*—being there in the workplace, attending meetings, and participating in daily activities. This visibility helps leaders stay connected with their team and understand the day-to-day realities of their work. Physical presence also demonstrates a leader's commitment and willingness to engage directly with their team [3].

Second, presence requires *emotional and intellectual engagement*. Leaders must actively listen to their team members, showing empathy and understanding. This means paying attention to both verbal and non-verbal cues, asking thoughtful questions, and providing constructive feedback. Emotional presence helps build trust and rapport, which are essential for effective leadership [4].

The benefits of presence in leadership are multifaceted. By being present, leaders can identify and address issues more effectively. They gain first-hand knowledge of the challenges faced by their team, which enables them to make more informed decisions. This understanding also enhances a leader's credibility, as team members are more likely to trust and respect leaders who have demonstrated a genuine interest in their work and well-being [5].

Additionally, presence fosters a sense of connection and support within the team. When leaders are visibly engaged, team members feel valued and understood. This can lead to higher levels of job satisfaction, motivation, and overall team performance.

Presence in leadership is particularly important during times of change or crisis. During these periods, teams look to their leaders for guidance and reassurance. A leader who is present and engaged can provide the stability and direction needed to navigate challenges effectively. Their presence helps to maintain morale, reduce uncertainty, and ensure that the team remains focused on achieving their goals [6].

Leaders should also make an effort to be approachable and accessible. This means being available to team members when they need support or have questions. Leaders can create an open-door policy, encouraging team members to come forward with their concerns and ideas. Being approachable helps to build trust and fosters open communication within the team [7].

The impact of presence in leadership extends beyond immediate interactions. Leaders who are consistently present set a positive example for their team. They model the behaviours and values that they expect from others, such as commitment, engagement, and respect. This modelling effect can influence team culture, promoting a more inclusive, collaborative, and motivated work environment [8].

Other Gems

1. *Schedule regular rounding in clinical areas and be consistent in your availability.* Regular, consistent interactions help build trust and ensure ongoing communication between leaders and their teams. This consistency demonstrates reliability and commitment.
2. *Engage with all members of the team, showing genuine interest in the work being done, offering assistance when necessary.* Leaders should feel comfortable participating in the work they expect of their team. This ensures that leaders lead from the front and lead by example.
3. Participating in operational activity within your team's environment, while demonstrating an authentic interest in daily operations helps leaders stay connected and informed about team dynamics and challenges.
4. *Be available to all members of the team, demonstrating active listening and empathy.* Both are crucial for building strong, positive relationships within the team. They help leaders understand team members' perspectives and foster a supportive environment.

References

1. Heifetz, R. A., & Laurie, D. L. (1997). The work of leadership. *Harvard Business Review, 75*(1), 124–134.
2. Goleman, D. (1998). What makes a leader? *Harvard Business Review.* http://fs.ncaa.org/Docs/DIII/What%20Makes%20a%20Leader.pdf
3. Kouzes, J. M., & Posner, B. Z. (2017). *The leadership challenge: How to make extraordinary things happen in organizations* (6th ed., Wiley). https://nibmehub.com/opac-service/pdf/read/The%20Leadership%20Challenge_%20How%20to%20Make%20Extraordinary%20Things%20Happen%20in%20Organizations.pdf
4. Gardner, W. L., Avolio, B. J., Luthans, F., May, D. R., & Walumbwa, F. (2005). Can you see the real me? A self-based model of authentic leader and follower development. *Leadership Quarterly, 16*(3), 343–372. https://digitalcommons.unl.edu/cgi/viewcontent.cgi?article=1167&context=managementfacpub
5. Yukl, G. (2013). *Leadership in organizations* (8th ed.). Pearson. https://nibmehub.com/opac-service/pdf/read/Leadership%20in%20Organizations%20by%20Gary%20Yukl.pdf
6. Kotter, J. P. (1996). *Leading change.* Harvard Business Review Press. https://heller.brandeis.edu//executive-education/maine-2023-2024/april-2023-chilingerian/friday-pm/leading-change.pdf
7. Covey, S. R. (1989). *The 7 habits of highly effective people: Powerful lessons in personal change.* Simon & Schuster. https://ati.dae.gov.in/ati12052021_1.pdf
8. Senge, P. M. (1990). *The fifth discipline: The art and practice of the learning organization.* Doubleday. https://www.academia.edu/88173789/The_fifth_discipline_The_art_and_practice_of_the_learning_organization_by_Peter_Senge_New_York_Doubleday_Currency_1990

My Suitcase Is Pink

Sara Barnes

Leadership Pearl

As leaders, it is important to remember that employees may have a wide range of personality traits and that their past experiences can affect how they respond to certain situations.

Scenario

Isaac walks into the organisation's medical leadership symposium knowing it is going to be a long day. He opts to sit at a back table so he can discreetly exit for a "toilet break" or stand up and march for a minute or two without drawing attention. Unfortunately, this idea is thwarted as soon as he enters. "No back tables to be used. We want you all up at the front so as you can interact" the convener bellows. His mind starts racing, worried about how he will contain himself for the next 8 hours. "Eight more hours" he keeps saying to himself. "Eight more hours, I can sit still and be present throughout." Then he sees it. There is paper on the desk. Excitedly he takes some sheets and starts doodling. This could work he thinks.

"No sorry, that paper is for the first activity" says the activity leader. Despair starts to creep in as he hands back the paper and pens. He starts tapping his own pen on the table and jiggling his leg as he tries to control his nervous energy.

Then the first activity is announced: "Mindfulness in meetings; how we can all strive to do better." His heart sinks. He sits still, noting he has already broken the

S. Barnes (✉)
Department of General Medicine, Department of Monash Health Lung, Sleep and Allergy, Monash Health, Melbourne, VIC, Australia

Monash University, Melbourne, VIC, Australia

R. Junckerstorff, S. Baqar (eds.), *Leadership Pearls in Healthcare*,
https://doi.org/10.1007/978-981-96-4233-5_45

rules; the pen tapping, the leg jiggling, the attempted doodling. I am breaking the mindfulness rules. Eye contact, look down. Only 7 more hours to go.

Discussion

Recognising that everyone has past experiences that may affect their future behaviour and interactions is important not only within the workplace but indeed in everyday life [1]. Whilst there are many resources discussing the benefit of being 'mindful in the moment' and using non-verbal tools, these may not be appropriate for everyone we interact with. In order to provide an inclusive and supportive environment, we need to consider the needs of people who may not recognise or respond to the "usual" cues and societal expectations [2]. This is true both in formal leadership tasks such as chairing a meeting where there are usually specific rules that are followed, but also in informal leadership roles and interactions [3]. An informal leader is a person who is well respected within a group but does not have a formal leadership title. An informal leader may not even be aware they hold this role, but the fact they are recognised by others as a leader, means their behaviour and opinions are held in high regard [2, 4].

As a leader, there are many different styles of communication that we need to consider for both ourselves and others. These may be related to culture, religion, neurodiversity or past lived experiences [3, 5]. There is often a focus on mindfulness in meetings, including being 'in the moment', and suggestions for posture, avoiding fidgeting, the role of eye contact and the importance of recognising non-verbal cues [3, 6]. The published literature both in peer reviewed journals and workplace training modules, defines meeting etiquette and acceptable workplace behaviour within a preconceived construct, with variance from these behaviours being deemed disrespectful [3, 5, 6].

When a person does not meet the local societal expectations, it is important to consider why and how as a leader you can help them to feel comfortable and included, as well as supporting the other members in the group who may feel disgruntled by the behaviour. It is important not to judge and reprimand in the first instance, however it is important to address these issues. When people feel that meeting behaviours are not being followed, how the group functions and the quality of the meeting can deteriorate.

Good leadership includes developing alternatives that improve inclusivity, for example, allowing for online typed questions, more flexible rules around devices that may also be utilised as fidget tools (e.g. phones are allowed in the room but please don't answer emails) and being compassionate to those who may struggle to verbally engage or maintain eye contact in the setting of a formal meeting or in required social events [3, 6]. Reach out to the person and discuss with them their needs and preferences. If you don't ask, you may never discover what could be helpful, nor how you can help facilitate a culture of inclusiveness [7, 8]. The impact of online virtual meetings in healthcare and their acceptability for individuals of various personality styles, neurodiversity or cultural backgrounds is not clear. For example, the accepted etiquette of always having one's camera on, may not be beneficial for individuals who struggle with eye contact. Similarly, having the flexibility to stand within a meeting allows those who need to fidget a discreet way of doing so. In the above scenario, if the convenor had quietly asked Isaac why he needed to sit in the back, a simple solution may have been found as well as other ways in which to help make the day a better learning experience for him and others in the session.

Other Gems

1. Leadership can be formal and informal. Simple actions including non-verbal cues can guide others on what is acceptable.
2. You never know unless you ask.

References

1. Price-Dowd, C. F. J. (2020). Your leadership style: Why understanding yourself matters. *BMJ Leader, 4*, 165–167.
2. Peters, L., & O'Conner, E. (2001, May–June). Informal leadership support: An often overlooked competitive advantage. *Physician Executive, 27*, 35–39.
3. Ferrar, M, & LaMeau, M. (2015). *Social skills*. Chapter: Workplace Etiquette and Conduct; Proper Meeting Etiquette. Farmington Hills, Gale part of Cengage.
4. Downey, M., Parslow, S., & Smart, M. (2011). The hidden treasure in nursing leadership: Informal leaders. *Journal of Nursing Management, 19*, 517–521.
5. Kemp, L., & Williams, P. (2013). In their own time and space: Meeting behaviour in the Gulf Arab workplace. *International Journal of Cross-Cultural Management, 13*(2).
6. De Jarnatt, C. (2008, January). Seven meeting etiquette rules not to forget. *Business Credit*.
7. Smith, T., & Kirby, A. (2021). *Neurodiversity at work*. Kogan Page.
8. Lehmann-Willenbrock, J., & Belyeu, A. (2016). Our love/hate relationship with meetings. *Management Research Review, 39*(10), 1293–1312.

Mastering the Art of Never Getting Angry

Nick Coatsworth

Leadership Pearl

Anger in a leadership position is rarely, if ever, a useful tool. In fact, it quickly erodes your leadership credibility and effectiveness. In my career, I can vividly recall the few times I became angry in professional situations. These instances were almost always associated with heightened stress and personal pressure.

Scenario

There were moments in my career, such as in the Congo with Médecins Sans Frontières (MSF) and during the COVID-19 pandemic, where the stress levels were immense, and the temptation to react with anger was strong. However, I have learned that losing one's temper never leads to a positive outcome. It damages relationships, undermines trust, and can derail productive discussions and decision-making processes. Maintaining composure, even in the face of extreme stress, is a hallmark of effective leadership.

Discussion

As a leader, it is not unusual that at times you will feel frustrated or angry. This is particularly likely when personal investment in an outcome is high. Clinicians are most familiar with these feelings during situations of inter-professional conflict for

N. Coatsworth (✉)
School of Regulation and Global Governance, Australian National University,
Canberra, ACT, Australia

example, when clinical recommendations differ between colleagues. The powerful sense of ownership and responsibility for a patient's safety can lead to emotions spilling over. Controlling our emotions ends up being a critical patient safety issue.

When you feel anger rising, it's essential to take a step back, reflect, and find ways to calm yourself. This might involve taking a brief break, focusing on the issue rather than the person, and practicing self-control. As simple as they sound, in the heat of the moment techniques such as deep breathing, mindfulness, and reflection can help manage emotions and maintain composure. It's important to remember that as leaders, our reactions set the tone for the entire team. A calm and measured response can defuse tense situations and foster a more collaborative environment.

The COVID-19 pandemic presented a unique set of challenges that tested my ability to remain calm under pressure. As Deputy Chief Medical Officer, I was frequently in the public eye, providing updates and guidance on the evolving situation. The high stakes and fast-paced environment were potential triggers for stress and frustration. However, I knew that any display of anger or frustration would undermine my credibility and the trust placed in me by the public and my colleagues. Maintaining a calm and composed demeanour was crucial in navigating the complexities of the pandemic response.

One of the key strategies I employed to manage stress and avoid anger was to prepare thoroughly for each engagement. By knowing the desired outcomes, anticipating potential challenges, and having a clear plan, I was better equipped to handle difficult situations without resorting to anger. This approach not only helped in maintaining my composure but also ensured that I could lead effectively and make informed decisions.

Another important aspect of managing anger is self-awareness. Understanding your triggers and recognising the signs of rising anger can help you take proactive steps to manage your emotions.

Very occasionally, a situation demands a controlled demonstration of displeasure. In situations I have seen this approach work, I am almost certain that the individual displaying the anger had prepared for the interaction and was using it to control the outcome. Although it's not a technique that I use, the key message is controlled displeasure, and do not under any circumstance lose that control.

In addition to self-awareness and self-control, having a support network is vital. During the COVID-19 pandemic, I relied on the support of my colleagues, family, and friends. Sharing my experiences, seeking advice, and simply having someone to talk to helped alleviate stress and provided a different perspective on challenging situations. I would often call friends and colleagues that I hadn't seen for months or even years just to 'chew the fat.' Clearly conversations with friends and colleagues should not breach confidence or be a forum for workplace gossip, however it is useful to have one or two very close colleagues to whom you can unconditionally vent feelings of frustration or anger.

Finally, it is essential to create a work environment that fosters open communication and mutual respect. Encouraging team members to express their concerns, providing constructive feedback, and addressing conflicts promptly can help prevent frustration and anger. In my leadership roles, I have always prioritised creating an environment where everyone feels heard and valued. This approach not only helps in managing my own emotions but also promotes a positive and collaborative team dynamic.

Ultimately, mastering the art of not getting angry enhances your ability to lead effectively. It builds a reputation for calmness, rationality, and fairness, which are essential qualities in a leader. By maintaining self-control, you can navigate challenging situations more effectively, build stronger relationships, and achieve better outcomes for your team and organisation.

Other Gems

1. Displays of anger are rarely, if ever, warranted in leadership roles and can rapidly undermine the confidence of your team.
2. Know your own triggers and have a series of go-to techniques to manage anger and frustration during interactions with colleagues.

Next Time It Could Be Me

Sara Barnes

Leadership Pearl

When an error or an adverse event occurs, it is important to fix the problem and not to affix blame.

Scenario

Nurse Robert opened the Electronic Medical Record to commence his medication round. It had been a quiet morning, which was unusual for the busy surgical ward he worked on. He did have several post-operative patients about to return to the ward in a short space of time and was concentrating on what he would need for their immediate post-operative care. Robert scanned the medications he needed. He asked Melissa to check the pain relief he was administering to his patient John who had just had a revision of his knee replacement. John promptly took all the oral medications with one gulp of water, not giving Melissa and Robert time to do the bedside check. Two hours later, Robert checked on John and found him to be unrousable. A Medical Emergency Team call was activated who treated John with naloxone (an antidote to narcotic pain relief), which led to a rapid improvement in his conscious state. Later at the end of their shift, Melissa and Robert did an inventory of the medications of addiction on the ward and realised that a potent narcotic pain killer was missing. Suddenly, the cause for John's altered conscious state became evident.

S. Barnes (✉)
Department of General Medicine, Department of Monash Health Lung, Sleep and Allergy, Monash Health, Melbourne, Australia

Monash University, Melbourne, Australia

After further investigation by the pharmacy department and the nursing leadership team, it was identified that these two medications had similar names and were stored right next to each other. The medication cupboard was re-sorted and medications with similar names were subsequently stored on separate shelves.

Discussion

When a mistake happens, the immediate facts will generally identify a person or an action preceding the event [1]. The person themselves may question what they have done and how they could have prevented this from occurring. Although being able to accept that you have made a mistake and acknowledge this shows humility and a growth mindset, it is often not the entire solution. Systems, processes, and culture all have a role in how and why errors occur [1, 2]. Placing the blame solely on an individual can create a culture within an organisation of fear and defensiveness. It can also prevent organisational growth and development [3].

Alexander Pope said that "to err is human, to forgive is divine", however, to acknowledge an error, to confess a mistake and to learn from it is divinely inspiring [4, 5]. Whether it is a fact that has been corrected or a poorly handled situation, how we as leaders handle our mistakes makes a significant impression on those around us [2]. It is often easy to acknowledge an error when it is a factual mistake, however, to understand, reflect and apologise when your own behaviour has not been what is required takes more humility and emotional control [2]. If you are informed of an error that you or someone else has made, be proud that you have been able to create a culture in which errors are able to be identified without fear of recrimination [3].

As demonstrated in the above scenario, when an error occurs it is not necessarily the first time it has occurred or nearly occurred. Reviewing the situation by stepping back and looking at the big picture can help identify more effective and lasting solutions [1]. By embracing a solution focused approach over blaming and shaming, communication, learning, development, and morale can be nurtured within an organisation. This enables growth not only of the people within the organisation, but of the of the organisation itself [3].

Other Gems

1. Leaders themselves need to acknowledge their own errors to enable transparency and to allow thoughtful, reflective problem solving.

References

1. Helmreich, R. (2000). On error management: Lessons from aviation. *BMJ, 320*(781).

2. Zhang, K., Zhao, B., & Yin, K. (2024). When leaders acknowledge their own errors, will employees follow suit? A social learning perspective. *Journal of Business Ethics, 189*, 403–421.
3. Frese, M., & Keith, N. (2015). Action errors, error management, and learning in organisations. *Annual Review of Psychology, 66.*
4. Pope, A. (1713). An essay on criticism accessed in Project Gutenberg August 25th 2024. https://www.gutenberg.org/cache/epub/7409/pg7409-images.html
5. Nichols, P., Copeland, T., Craib, I., Hopkins, P., & Bruce, D. (2008). Leading from error: Identifying contributory causes of medication errors in an Australian Hospital. *MJA.*

Making the Choice to Lead

Nick Coatsworth

Leadership Pearl

Choosing to lead is the most impactful decision I've made in my career. Leadership, especially in the demanding and high-stakes environment of healthcare, transcends titles; it's about shouldering the responsibility to guide, influence, and inspire others.

Situation

Over the past decades, I've held various medical leadership roles that have shaped my understanding of leadership. Whether it be a hospital leadership role, serving as President of the Australian Chapter of Médecins Sans Frontières (MSF) or stepping into the role of Deputy Chief Medical Officer of Australia during the early COVID-19 pandemic, I've learned that leadership isn't defined by titles but by daily actions in the operational environment. Each role, though significant, highlighted the importance of everyday leadership in practical settings, emphasising the need to lead by example, inspire trust, and foster collaboration among colleagues.

Discussion

A common criticism in healthcare today is the prevalence of non-physician administrators in leadership roles, including nurses, full-time health administrators, and allied health professionals. Some doctors view this lack of medical leadership as a

N. Coatsworth (✉)
School of Regulation and Global Governance, Australian National University,
Canberra, ACT, Australia

problem and seize the opportunity to criticise. However, this perspective abdicates our responsibility. Dating back to Hippocrates, medical professionals have the longest heritage of any health profession. In clinical environments, whether in team meetings, discussions about hospital restructuring, or planning a new hospital, we benefit from this historical privilege. This brings with it a responsibility to lead.

The heritage and tradition associated with medical leadership underscore a deeper responsibility that medical professionals carry. Our training, experience, and understanding of clinical intricacies position us uniquely to lead effectively in healthcare environments. However, we can't rely on that heritage and expect to be listened to simply by virtue of being doctors.

If doctors aren't leading within the healthcare environment or if we're concerned that other professionals are taking on leadership roles, we have only ourselves to blame. This means actively seeking opportunities to guide, influence, and support our colleagues and the healthcare system. It also means avoiding criticising health professionals who choose to lead, especially if we haven't made that choice ourselves. By stepping up and taking on leadership roles, we can drive the changes we want to see in the healthcare system, ensuring that it remains patient-centred and clinically driven.

Choosing to lead in challenging environments brings some unique benefits. My role as a field doctor for MSF in the Republic of Congo, Chad, and Sudan involved leading local staff who were far more aware of the local context and the operating environment than I was. They taught me that leadership is not about being the loudest voice in the room but about being the most attentive listener, the most thoughtful planner, and the most reliable team member.

Choosing to lead involves a deep commitment to continuous personal growth. Great leaders are lifelong learners who constantly seek to improve themselves and their skills. This principle is especially important in healthcare, where the landscape is constantly evolving, and leaders must stay ahead of new developments, technologies, and best practices. Continuous learning involves not just staying updated with the latest clinical guidelines and treatments but also understanding healthcare management, policy changes, and innovations in patient care. It's about being versatile and adaptable, ready to meet the demands of a dynamic healthcare environment.

Other Gems

1. Leadership in medicine is a choice and by corollary we can choose not to lead, but if we make the latter choice, be cautious criticising the leaders.
2. Use the heritage of medical leadership to positive effect. Doctors will always be seen as the leaders of the multi-disciplinary team. Be responsible with that heritage.
3. Realise the benefits of choosing to lead, whether it is enhanced resilience in complex environments or lifelong personal growth.

The manufacturer's authorised representative in the EU is Springer
Nature Customer Service Centre GmbH, Europaplatz 3, 69115 Heidelberg,
Germany. If you have any concerns regarding our products, please
contact ProductSafety@springernature.com

Printed and bound by CPI Group (UK) Ltd, Croydon, CR0 4YY

27/04/2026

02097605-0002